Ben Baker's Christmas Box

Forty years of the best, worst and weirdest Christmas TV

Ben Baker

First published in Great Britain in 2021

By Ben Baker Books

www.benbakerbooks.org

The book author retains sole copyright to their contributions to this book. All rights reserved. No part of this publication may be reproduced or transmitted in any form or by any means, electronically or mechanically, including photocopying, recording or any information storage of retrieval system without either prior permission in writing from the publisher. So, no copying it on Betamax tape for all yer mates! Especially you Curran.

Copyright All Text 2017-2021 Ben Baker

Printed by Lulu Press

Find me on Twitter @Benbakerbooks

*"Let's all sing the Christmas medley /
switch off the hi-fi / switch off the TV…"*

Contents

Introduction 5

For Kids Of All Ages 9
Hey! A Movie! The Sixties 26
Pop Is Quite Top 37
The Ballad of Noel Edmonds 57
So Much Drama 65
Only Fools and Ratings 80
That Thing You Like But Ten Minutes Longer 89
Hey! A Movie! The Seventies 97
Queen's Greatest Hits 109
Lenny Henry: The True Spirit of Christmas? 117
Game For A Quiz 126
Hey! A Movie! The Eighties 138
Sketchy People 153
Muppetational Moments 175
Hey! A Movie! The Nineties 183
New Year's Daze 198

Closedown 233
Other Books What I Done 235

Introduction

As a man who has written three books about Christmas television in the UK, you'd expect I'd be sick to the sprout-flecked teeth of the subject right now.

The first – "Festive Double Issue" was a fleeting sweep through the chunky Radio and TV Times of old, picking out things that sounded exciting, different or just plain weird. Much of it was lost media and so a lot of the book ended up being giddy speculation about the contents and sharing them with readers like a kid with a new 'Bleeping Alan' on Christmas Day. With that itch scratched I moved onto other projects…and yet it still danced in the tinsel-decked caverns of my mind - often to the tune of The Futureheads' "Christmas Was Better in the 80s" a rare modern seasonal song that was actually both excellent and not a maudlin jingle bell-swamped cover version slowed by 200%.

With that title as my jumping off point I focused in on the decade of MTV, My Pet Monster and Michael Jackson before, you know, the stuff. As well as things beginning with M I tried to offer a thoroughly UK-based perspective on the last week of December and there are few, if any, books about that decade that would devote time to the disparate likes of the **"Hale and Pace Christmas Extravaganda"** (9pm, Channel 4, December 20th 1986), **"Terry Wogan in Pantoland"** (7pm, BBC One, December 21st 1988) with Peter Powell or **"Russ Abbot's Hogmanay Madhouse"** (8pm, ITV, December 31st 1982). Whether anyone needed that was another question but on release it sold even better than the first book. Not Madhouse-mortgaging amounts but enough to keep me in Eggnog and bins to throw all that Eggnog in over Christmas 2019. I definitely decided there and then though I was absolutely, positively not going to write another book about festive telly. I didn't want to be the "Christmas Book Guy" and also didn't want to bore people with more of the same year after year.

And then 2020 happened.

Suddenly the world was thrown into a maelstrom of new, confusing and genuinely terrifying things. To try and get through the days locked down and isolated from loved ones many turned to those good old staples of British life: booze and telly. At first the likes of "Tiger King", "Normal People" or Joe Wicks suggesting we might like to move around a bit were good distraction but as the weeks dragged on and we spent more collective time sat on our bums in the house, folk started to yearn for some comfort via media from a simpler, non-hideously mutated time. Stuff we'd seen, heard or read hundreds of times before. Cinemas, when allowed to open, ran "Grease", "Hocus Pocus" and "Back to The Future" to appreciative crowds. Come December 2020, the top forty was crammed with old Christmas songs giving two previous No.2 hits – "Last Christmas" and "All I Want for Christmas Is You" - their first run at the top spot. BBC One responded by filling some of their now-empty slots with repeats of "Blackadder II", "Gavin and Stacey" and "Fawlty Towers".

The fact the major channels managed to get anything new on screen at all over the holidays felt like a small miracle – not that it stopped people moaning about too many Gruffalos stealing our jobs or summat – but knowing there was a festive schedule full of recognisable properties, be they "Call the Midwife", "The Chase" or A Shrek, was a comfort to many.

As such, it was that world I flung "I Was Bored on Christmas Day" which was my attempt to provide a bit of much needed nostalgia while also tracking how television had changed over the course of the 1990s with the rise of satellite TV, 24-hour programming and even a fifth terrestrial channel which some people say is even still going. It was a hard book to write and I definitely went mad at least once writing it but I'm proud of finally putting my Christmas TV trilogy to bed.

So why am I still here?

Ziggy says there's a 95% chance I'm here to present some of my favourite bits from those three books, totally reworked and updated, along with some new chapters and lots of my favourite stories. I really did set out to do a standard 'best of' for a wider audience who might not care about the difference between ITV regions or what time The Grimleys was on. But as I compiled the book, I started to notice lots of things that connected together and programmes I'd missed the first time round or had since emerged on YouTube or definitely not shady at all private members-only websites[1]. There's a guide to every major film shown on Christmas Day since 1960 now, plus what the channels did on New Year's Eve too.

This isn't an exhaustive compilation of programming and I've mostly left some of the more obvious fayre such as Morecambe and Wise, James Bond films and "Top of The Pops" because they've been covered so many times by people far more knowledgeable about those subjects. I'm far more interested in the things that slipped between the cracks of our

---

[1] This sounds like old episodes of "Bruce Forsyth's Generation Game" were dancing in cages for money but I really don't need you to have that image in your head. It's there already? Oh. Sorry about that.

collective memories from the once huge programmes that have been lost in time through changing attitudes or simply not existing to view in the modern era anymore to the oddities that snuck out when people were incapacitated by turkey and wine. Shows with unusual time lengths that took advantage of the looser Christmas schedules or were the counterprogramming to some of the behemoths that get all the attention because of ratings and stars.

It's a fascinating area to research as it really does reflect everything going on in the country at any given time from stars to politics. From black and white to colour, from two channels to two hundred, Christmas TV is the celebration of being together and sharing an experience at the same time. It reflects the best and occasionally worst of Britain but it is quintessentially a British tradition. You only have to look at all the Australians on the beach or America chucking out their big seasonal specials around the 10th of December to see that we're still suckers for the old way of doing things.

Therefore, am I sick of writing about Christmas TV? Not for a second. But this really is the very final, last ever, definitive word on the subject and I will not be swayed by you buying hundreds of copies of this book and telling all your friends about it. Absolutely not. No sir.

See you next year then?

Ben Baker,

the majestic beaches of Keighley tarn, October 2021

For Kids of All Ages

"We do it all for the kiddies, don't we?" your sweaty uncle George says as he opens his sixth can of ALDI high-strength lager and steps on the Scalextric set. It certainly was true of television many years ago with its constant cycle of circuses and pantomimes but in our corner of the 21st century Christmas is one of the few times you might actually see a festive special for younger viewers thanks to the major networks farming off everything to their own digital channels. In their place there's a heavier reliance on recent animated movie repeats and, on BBC One, the now traditional big new Christmas Day short film based inevitably on a kids book with twelve pages and a cute furry monster called Plemp. Admittedly, its infinitely better than having to sit through fifteen hours of boring dubbed drama from Switzerland about a dull boy and his magical goose but seeing something like "Why Don't You?" or "Junior Kick Start" on the listings page always felt like Christmas had truly arrived.

Admittedly most of us over the age of fifteen without children or standards rarely see anything before midday on Christmas and for the longest time telly reflected that with the BBC starting up around half past nine and the commercial channel an hour or so later. And even when it did wobble onto air it was only really religion allowed before twelve plus the odd carol service and sick child being visited by later disgraced celebrities in hospital. By the turn of the eighties, television still didn't much bother rolling out of its scratcher before "Play School" and that lazy young Channel 4 barely made on air for the afternoon, no doubt stinking of booze and fags from the night before.

But as January 1983 jogged into view so too did the first nationwide breakfast television transmissions with the BBC's

"Breakfast Time" going head-to-head with "TV-am" each weekday morning and causing a huge stir with people blissfully unaware it would lead to an increase of Piers Morgan's face. Suddenly there was telly for those businessmen in their suit and tie who had been up since 5am, bored homeworkers and their yawning schoolkids to train their one open eye onto. And nobody split the room more than a ratty puppet named Roland.

It's a story that's been written many a time about how Roland Rat's "Spectacular Shedvision Show" segments effectively saved TV-am from its initial low viewership (*"rat joins sinking ship ha ha"*, copyright Every Newspaper Ever) but, with the full support of new Editor-in-Chief Greg Dyke and future Ragdoll Productions[2] supremo Anne Wood, it's not hard to see why. David Claridge's puppet was genuinely modern for the times, could interact wittily with humans around him and was as obsessed with celebrity as many of his young fans who rushed out to buy his dolls, games, books and even the truly awful "Rat Rapping" single.

Starting on December 19th 1983 and running right through to January, **"Roland's Winter Wonderland"** was the second opportunity to break the increasingly popular puppet out of the confines of TV-am's Camden Lock studios after the incredibly successful "Rat on the Road" took the superstar rat and his sidekick Kevin the Gerbil around the UK in his trademark pink Ford Anglia "Ratmobile". For Christmas '83 the same characters headed slightly further afield for a trip to Switzerland, now joined by put-upon Welsh miserabilist Errol

---

[2] Makers of shows like Teletubbies, Rosie and Jim, In the Night Garden and at the very start, a little wooden kid in a pink and yellow jumper who we'll be meeting in a few pages….

the Hamster. Easter 1984 saw them travel even further to Hong Kong for "Roland Goes East" hindered by Roland's hyperactive stowaway brother Little Reggie. "TOILET!"

Roland would famously burrow out of breakfast TV and onto the BBC in a controversial transfer the year after. Broadcast on Christmas Day, **"Roland's Yuletide Binge"** (11:30am, BBC One, 1985) would announce his glittering arrival at the new gaff with a fun wander around the studios bumping into various stars of the time including Russell Grant, Ian McCaskill, Frankie Howerd, Beryl Reid and Jan 'Lemming' Leeming in the news room. Thanks in part to a script co-written by Richard Curtis, it's funny and just about stretches to its 25-minute length but lacks the spontaneity and surprise of his earlier breakfast outings with unsuspecting celebrities who were less in on the joke. By the time "Roland Rat – The Series" appeared on Saturday evenings in September 1986 the joke felt already worn thin and by the following Christmas Day's special he was moved back to the slightly earlier time of 8.45am.

He wouldn't be the only bin-raiding puppet animal to get a BBC One series. Truly, he was a mere fly by night when compared to the back catalogue of apparently aristocratic fox Basil Brush who had been a staple of the snow topped schedules after becoming a popular part of magician David Nixon's shows for the channel. His first Christmas Day appearance was 1970's **"Basil's Christmas Morning"** when Mr Derek was still on the payroll. 1971s **"Basil in Pantoland"** was followed by **Basil Brush's Christmas Fantasy** (December 22nd, 1974) **"Basil's Christmas in Norway"** (December 20th, 1975), **"Basil in Neverland"** (December 18th, 1976) and **"Basil's Christmas in the**

Country" (December 22nd, 1979) but only **"Basil Through the Looking Glass"** in 1977 would get the prime Christmas Day placing with **"Basil's Christmas Cruise"** (December 27th, 1980) being his last solo programme for the channel until the 2002 revival. A sad indictment of the fickle British public. Although mainly limited to the popularity of TV puppet foxes admittedly.

Basil's rise as the Corporation's chief puppet funster was certainly helped by the defection of a fellow entertainer that had made its name on the BBC going before going over to the commercial channel for the riches and glory. Clips from both the BBC and Thames eras would therefore appear in **"The Sooty Story – The First 30 Years"** (4:45pm, ITV, 29th December 1983) which mixed interviews with both mildly confused real people (*"He played the piano...no, the xylophone!"*; *"I remember Ronnie Corbett was presenting it..."*) and celebrities...well, Bonnie Langford anyway. Despite these comic overtones, it's actually a fairly straight documentary featuring both Harry Corbett and son Matthew – who at one point can be seen composing on TWO KEYBOARDS AT THE SAME TIME!!! in his home recording studio making him look seriously rock 'n' roll - alongside behind-the-scenes footage revealing how good the Corbetts were with both puppetry and their interaction with audiences. Despite this Sooty felt like a product of a very different time compared to the likes of Roland Rat or Pob, the Gove-faced wooden puppet who supposedly lived inside the viewer's television.

"Pob's Christmas Special" (2pm, Channel 4, December 24th 1986) was much the same as any other episode of "Pob's Programme" with its jaunty parping theme tune, celebrities – in this edition the then-ubiquitous comedy actress Su Pollard - following unravelling coloured jumper strings to rhyming clues, Dick King Smith's boring inserts with his dog, cartoons, crafts, the "naughty teddy" and Pob cleaning the end credits off the inside of your TV screen all etched in the mind of a particular generation so vividly that it's a surprise that there's barely a scrap of "Pob's Programme" or many of Channel 4's excellent early kids shows anywhere in the internet bar people mentioning the many complaints over Pob's "spitting".

Equally upsetting to the sensitive nature of some adults, although thankfully more represented online thanks to its fans, was the wild, messy Saturday morning programme **"Tiswas"** which had grown from a small Midlands-only broadcast to the majority of the UK, becoming a home for the disparate likes of Frank Carson, Lenny Henry and Bob Carolgees along with regular presenters Chris Tarrant and Sally James. It was a space where bands like The Clash and Motorhead popped in because it was a laugh with comedy guests such as Terry Jones turning up to promote "Life of Brian" a film none of the target audience could actually go and see. All of this led to its reputation as the cool thing to be watching and the Christmas show from 22nd December 1979 would feature a party every kid worth his large seventies' trousers wanted to attend with bands, comedy, flans and even a live cow in the studio! The cast ran through the obligatory "A Christmas Carol" parody with former Scaffold member John Gorman as the miserable miser while Bob, Sally, comedian Norman Collier and RADA's very own Spit the Dog play to the crowd as the poor "Family Scratchspit". "Christmas Compost Corner" (barely) contained Carson in full terrible gag flow to the delight of himself if not necessarily the assembled kids and there was music from the comedy pop act The Barron Knights who were back in the charts after a welcome break.

The following year would see the series skyrocket even more in both popularity and quality so few were surprised when it was announced everyone bar James would be off to conquer late night adult TV in the ambitious but incredibly patchy live comedy "OTT". Saturday mornings would take years to recover and many would agree that nobody came close to the outright kid-adored lunacy until "Dick and Dom In Da Bungalow" two decades later. That had caused uproar too at the time in part because the BBC were usually the home of generally safer gunge-free affairs like "Multi-Coloured Swap Shop" and "Saturday Superstore".

Their successor "Going Live!" was also largely muck muck free preferring instead to gently remix all the best features from those earlier shows with more personality and, like Tarrant and Co before, a huge increase in comedy. Not only were hosts Phillip Schofield and Sarah Greene very in sync and very witty they were joined each week (except that one series we don't talk about) by the double act Trevor and Simon who would appear every half hour or so with a series of silly characters like the dodgy Sister Brothers, sixties throwbacks The Singing Corner, the not very spooky World of the Strange and DJ Mick McMac ("the man with the mix!") and the Bez-esque acid casualty Moon Monkey, hosts of the Pot Fish Rave Club. To give the series a bit of time off over Christmas, "Going Live!" would become **"Gone Live!"**

Initially a bit of filler between the cartoons and pop promos, these had even more emphasis on the sketches and New Year's Eve 1988's edition found the team travelling through various time periods between links. Come the year after it had expanded to a full-on pantomime featuring cameos by a microcosm of everyone who'd been successful or noteworthy that year. Suitably, **"Philderella"** (9am, December 30th 1989) featured the unlikely combination of comedian Helen Lederer, singer Sydney Youngblood actors Vas Blackwood and Christopher Ryan plus members from pop acts And Why Not, London Boys, Big Fun and Brother Beyond. **"Scrooge - A Christmas Sarah"** (8:45am, December 29th 1990) brought in Rowland Rivron, Norman Lovett, Susie Blake and Normski as the four ghosts.

The panto theme was always a strong hatstand in which to balance a festive episode as everyone from "Crackerjack" to "The World at War" getting in on the act. The **"Rainbow Christmas Special"** (9:35am, ITV, December 26th 1986) ditched the usual mildly educational format for an adventure with *"George the Rainbow fairy to make sure all's well that ends well."* Stop that giggling as we're off to "Rainbow Town" with a tune by regular musical trio Rod, Jane and Freddy before Dame Bungle Bear crashes her bicycle and performs some classic comic woofers *("What a nice dress...satin?", "No, slept in")* Wide-mouthed irritant Zippy is the Panto's natural villain whose grand plan involves turning everything black and white. It's up to the Dame's son Geoffrey (try not to think too hard about that ungodly sexual union…) to claim back all the colours in the rainbow one by one through a series of legitimately creepy sets full of disembodied mouths and trees with faces like a deleted level on CITV's "Knightmare". The whole thing ends with Zippy casting one final spell: *"Chuckles, laughter, smiles and titters / I've put a rainbow on yer knickers..."* which Dame Bungle bends over and duly shows.

Any poor hung-over parents tuned in that morning must have wondered who'd spiked their turkey the previous evening. Equally inept but more committed to the cause was the titular baddy in **"T-Bag's Christmas Cracker"** (9:25am, ITV, December 27th 1988) where a plot to intercept Santa and swap his gifts for mind-control devices involves travelling back in time to the home of an Edwardian family and pretending to be a nanny called...cough, "Merry Pippins". The first of four seasonal one-offs for Lee Pressman and Grant Cathro's Tallulah Bag[3] and her press-ganged sidekick Thomas "T-" Shirt (John Hasler), this was a short and sweet one off compared to the character's usual longer serialised format – all of which invariably involved some torturous puns over the letter T. Speaking of which…

"Mr T's Christmas Dream" (11am, ITV, 21st December 1985) sold itself as a "heart-warming fantasy tale highlighted by music, magic and comedy" and delivered…well, mixed results. The one-off special had been broadcast first the previous year in the US as "Mr T & Emmanuel Lewis in A Christmas Dream" on NBC but as nobody here knew his tiny co-star - the 13-year-old Emmanuel Lewis from sickly 80s family sitcom "Webster"[4] – he was unceremoniously ditched from the UK title. What follows is a weird fantasy drama in which Mr T, still bringing in bumper ratings for ITV as part of gun-heavy action comedy "The A Team", plays a Salvation Army Santa who tries to cheer up a grumpy kid that has

---

3   Initially played by Elizabeth Estensen, she was replaced in 1990 by Georgina Hale as her sister Tabatha.

4   In which a black kid who loses his parents goes to live with a wealthy white family. No, it's not like Diff'rent Strokes. Because. Reasons.

stopped believing in Christmas by taking him to the gigantic toy store FAO Schwarz for a not at all sponsored segment that just happens to feature all the era's latest toys. David Copperfield is there too - the creepy magician one, sadly. Speaking of creepy, there's also seen-to-be-believed Willie Tyler and Lester at Radio City Music Hall.

It all ends at a random Christmas party at which Mr BA Barracus from "Rocky 3" tells the story of Baby Jesus' birth. Sort of. It's so rambling and barely coherent (One sample: *"Theologians...scholars...even, the prophets, not one of them can tell us if that baby smiled...we should help somebody who needs help because the blessed of us must try to save the less of us and then, and only then, will we know we have made that baby smile."*) that it smacks strongly of Mr T being given some sort of control over the script. And despite his many words, he didn't once mention going on no plane.

The special is a prime example of the sort of mad ideas that TV seemed willing to throw at a screen in the 1980s on the off-chance of a hit. And yet whilst that was doomed to be locked in the era it was created, the timeless **"A Charlie Brown Christmas"** (4:10pm, ITV, December 28th 1970) is still an absolute joy almost six decades after its creation. Produced in 1965 for CBS in America this was the first time a TV episode had brought the characters from Charles Shultz's insanely popular Peanuts comic strip to life. What could be a schmaltzy mess is instead a funny, truthful take on how different people - or, in this case, surprisingly erudite eight-year-olds - feel about the holidays. Naturally, there's some good old-fashioned slices of American cheese in there – the kids all singing 'Hark! The Herald Angels Sing!" around Charlie's awful Christmas tree for example – and even a bit of religion courtesy of Linus quoting the Gospel of Luke but it never feels preachy or forced. Best of all is the largely instrumental jazz soundtrack by the Vince Guaraldi Trio which remains one of those rare records that just radiates festive feeling in every note. "A Charlie Brown Christmas" remains a seasonal staple in America running every year on free television…until 2020 when Apple TV bought it for streaming only. The outcry was so huge they eventually relented and handed it over to free PBS stations with only minor sponsorship interference. Good grief!

With the Peanuts gang being such a success in 1965, the following year CBS would repeat their luck with another cartoon adaptation that also has endured for nearly sixty years. Undoubtedly better known in the UK since the Jim Carrey live-action remake, Dr Seuss' **"How the Grinch Stole Christmas"** (5:50pm, BBC Two, December 24th 1967) far outstrips that version with memorable music (in particular "You're A Mean One Mr Grinch" performed with great snarky menace by Thurl Ravenscroft), a perfectly pitched narration from a 79-year-old Boris Karloff and gorgeous artwork directed by the former Warner Bros legend Chuck Jones. Nine years later, CBS would also later commission **"Chuck Jones' Mowgli's Brothers"** (11:30am, ITV, 31st December 1987) which featured the animator's take on the first chapter of "The Jungle Book". Now, the animation scholars of you out there may be aware that the Disney corporation also made a version of this same obscure Rudyard Kipling story in 1967 and thus some scepticism is understandable when approaching. The all too brief 25-minute running time means there's no time for anything but the important beats of the story with Mowgli jumping from baby to boy as the simmering tension between the wolf packs and the wicked Shere Khan grows ever stronger. Jones' distinctive animation style is more noticeable in some areas over others but the use of colours and shadows make the story really stand out from the more familiar Disney take. Roddy McDowall provides all the male voices and gives the production a gravitas it deserves. Despite looking like one of those Poundland knock-offs from the outset it's a richer, more exciting take on the jungle tale and it would've been fascinating to see Chuck continue on to do the whole novel. Long a giant amongst his contemporaries, Jones would later be the subject of a ten-part BBC Two retrospective series **"What's Up Chuck?"** throughout Christmas 1985 with focus on different parts of his work including the importance of music and sound, staging and character development. Special episodes were also devoted to his work on Bugs Bunny, Daffy Duck, Roadrunner and Wile E Coyote.

Of course, we could still produce our own cartoon classics and Channel Four's **"The Snowman"** remains one of the very best. Originally shown on Boxing Day 1982, author Raymond Briggs introduced his own dialogue-free tale of a little boy and his flying frozen water-based acquaintance to a respectable viewership of 1.70m on the brand-new channel. "Hang on, where's the Thin White Duke?", you may be asking. Well, the more famous David Bowie opening was only added in 1983, a year he'd seemingly been everywhere thanks to the "Let's Dance" album and its three huge hit singles, to try and get interest from American broadcasters. Dianne Jackson's Oscar nominated[5] animation full of hand

---

[5] It lost the Academy Award for Best Animated Short Film to "Tango" by Zbigniew Rybczyński who would go on to direct music

drawn pastel-shaded art is still stunning all these years on and even though the original story had nothing to do with Christmas, it's still a huge part of Four's festive schedules long after the rest of the station went rubbish, peaking with 6 million viewers in 1985 and most often these days joined by its thirtieth anniversary sequel **"The Snowman and the Snowdog"** from 2012. And if everyone has been really good, we'll get a showing of Briggs' **"Father Christmas"** (5:45pm, Channel 4, December 24th 1991) too!

Written before "The Snowman"[6], it's a much funnier and cheekier film than its predecessor with the much-missed Mel Smith perfectly cast as the voice of the grumpy but good-hearted title character harrumphing and pottering through his suburban British house after yet another successful Christmas run. Viewers are then allowed to peak into what he does for the rest of the year which includes building a flying camper van to take him on a series of holidays including France where none of the food agrees with him leading to a series of comical needs to visit the toilet, a freezing cold dip in Scotland and getting cleaned out by a casino in Las Vegas.

After that it's time to go through the children's letters to gauge the presents needed before it's all systems go for Christmas Eve again. He still finds time to make it to the famous snowman's party as seen in the earlier animation though. *"Glad you could make it again...the party, not yer*

---

videos for everyone from Cameo to the Pet Shop Boys throughout the eighties.

6   This half hour is based on two of Briggs' books: "Father Christmas" (1973) and "Father Christmas Goes on Holiday" (1975) "The Snowman" was first published in 1978.

snowman!" says our jolly hero rather casually to the young boy from "The Snowman" as if he's not retro-fitting a happier ending to the previous tale after nearly a decade of tears!

The animation is as gorgeous as its predecessor, particularly as Father Christmas fights his way through the howling snow, crawling through chimneys and getting caught on TV aerials during his Christmas Eve manoeuvres. A brief dream sequence where the big man is haunted by monstrous versions of the foodstuff he's eaten in excess is also wonderfully odd. It may be less famous than some of his other book adaptations because it's incredibly British in its core – although that never stopped Wallace and Gromit from universal domination I suppose. Much like Briggs' beloved characters, it doesn't feel like Christmas without a bit of Wallace and Gromit who the BBC loved so much they even based a series of Christmas idents around in 1995. Thus, it might surprise some to learn that their first adventure **"A Grand Day Out"** (6pm, December 24th 1990) actually first appeared on Channel 4.

Nick Park's painstakingly produced student film about a man and his dog popping up to the moon for some cheese in the days before Uber Eats had been started in 1982 but due to taking other work for the growing Aardman studio would only be completed in 1989 to the point that even Peter Sallis had completely forgotten he'd recorded his part for it. "A Grand Day Out" was nominated for Best Animated Short Film at the 1990 Academy Awards but was sadly beaten by "Creature Comforts" made by...um, Nick Park.

Equally British in its sense of humour was **"Willo the Wisp"** (5:30pm, BBC One, 24th December 1981) which featured daft tales about the unusual inhabitants of Doyley Woods narrated by a spirit that had more than a passing resemblance to Kenneth Williams. Despite seemingly being on forever in my childhood, only 25 five-minute episodes were produced between September and November 1981. "Christmas Box" was to be the 26th and final episode concluding the series in which overweight fairy Mavis Cruet and Tony Hancock-esque know-all caterpillar Arthur believe the malevolent television set Evil Edna has turned Santa Claus into a big red frog. In terms of quality baddie, Edna is perhaps only beaten by Skeletor…until you actually go back and see any of the cartoons he came from like "**He-Man and She-Ra: A Christmas Special**" (4:15pm, ITV, 30th December 1985)

As an adult it's easy to see just how unashamed the eighties' cartoons had become at directly advertising toys at the under 10s. Better ask for all 372 characters and their variant models and big plastic box vaguely looking like a castle to shove them in or you may as well not turn up for school tomorrow, kids! "He-Man and the Masters of the Universe" and the female targeted spin-off "She-Ra: Princess of Power" were two of the worst offenders with bad animation, boring stories and really irritating characters. One such pain in the arse is Orko, a flying magic… thing, who is the catalyst for this story when a rocket sends him from usual setting Eternia to our very own Earth where he learns all about Christmas from some conveniently placed children. But not to worry – here's rotten old Skeletor to mess up He Man's plans and… wait, is he being licked by a robot puppy? He is. And he's…smiling!?! Goddamnit, you ruined Skeletor. And you don't even make a joke about him being made of bones! *"Blast it! I don't know what's coming over me... but whatever it is, I don't like it!"* You said it Skeletor mate.

Only mildly less awful was **"Yogi Bear's All-Star Comedy Christmas Caper"** (4:10pm, BBC One, 23rd December 1986) produced long into Hanna-Barbera's "will this do?" period. The script by legendary TV and comic writer Mark Evanier is fun enough (one toy reads "Super-Duper Ray Demolisher - be the first kid on your block to level Detroit!") but Yogi is such a hard character to find anything original to do with. Hence a change of location in this one-off allowing him and short-legged companion Boo Boo to sneak off into the 'Big City' where they dress as Santa and try cheer up a little girl with an ignorant businessman daddy while evading men with nets because…y'know, they are still bears loose in an urban environment. Lots of other Hanna-Barbera characters turn up along the way including Fred Flintstone and Barney Rubble whose appearance in the modern world is fairly questioned (*"a little far from Bedrock - like about three million years..."*) but never explained. Eventually lessons are learned, Christmases are merried and Yogi evades capture by the man for another day. With all the characters - including a horse, a dog, some mice, a gorilla and whatever Snagglepuss is meant to be – all sharing space here, quite why some animals are free to walk around and have jobs yet the bears are forbidden to leave the park is never addressed.

And we close this chapter with perhaps the one producer of family films that I haven't yet touched upon – no, not your dad with a camcorder trying to get £250 out of "You've Been Framed" – Disney who were represented for many years on British television by the long running BBC festive staple **"Disney Time"** beginning on Christmas Day 1964. The format was simple enough, a famous face would introduce a rare pre-VHS chance to see bits from varied House of Mouse productions, both animated and live-action, when Disney was the exclusive domain of the cinemas. For the inaugural edition, Julie Andrews – at that time starring in Disney's own "Mary Poppins" which was less than a week old in UK cinemas – linked an eclectic mix of clippage with the famous ("Lady and the Tramp", "Peter Pan") with the markedly less so ("The Legend of Lobo", "Those Calloways") Subsequent editions, often twice a year with a second programme at Easter or on a bank holiday, would be less bothered how connected to Disney the presenter was with French cabaret star Maurice Chevalier stepping up next, followed by the dart-in-a-board casting likes of Val Doonican (1968), Harry Worth (1969), Paul and Linda McCartney (1973), Derek Nimmo (1974), Marti Caine (1980), Windsor Davies (1981), Jan Francis (1985) and Kenny Everett (1987). The very final edition in 1995 was hosted by Michaela Strachan who fittingly saw in the next age of animation – and the future of Christmas week scheduling - with a preview of the all new "Toy Story". To infinity and wossname!

Hey! A Movie! The Sixties

Now I may be speaking out of turn here but I'm fairly sure everyone has seen a film. Some might have even seen two.

But actually, when you google "the films" it turns out there have been loads of them…easily over a thousand. And Christmas offers a perfect opportunity to catch up on both certified classics and newer releases that you might have missed at the pictures. Not surprisingly, in this age of instant streaming and new films simultaneously being released online the idea of a "big Christmas Day" movie is less of a draw as it once was. In recent years the latest Pixar film has taken the coveted post-Queen's speech slot around 3:10pm on BBC One while ITV have largely stopped bothering, preferring instead to rely on a range of homegrown formats like "The Chase", "Beat the Chasers", "The Chase Celebrity Special" and "Tipping Point…Oh no wait, it's Another Episode of The Chase". And yet when the festive schedules are posted online – perhaps the modern equivalent of ringing shows in the Radio Times - we all still excitedly check to see what is premiering where. And then tweet "OMG Seen it. Defund all BBCs immediately." Maybe.

Accordingly, this chapter is devoted to a look back at the rise and fall of 'the big Christmas Day movie' from 1960 to 1999. There'll be several Bonds, a number of escapees from the Disney Vault and a few genuine headscratchers that have been lost to time. There'll be something for the kiddies at lunchtime, a big family film after the Queen at 3pm to digest the dinner – slash fall asleep – to and possibly a big budget action spectacular in the evening if it was a year there was no Morecambe and Wise or Ronnie Barker was having a dump. I'll see you…at the movies*!!!!! (*next page)

1960

With radio still the choice of many households as the sixties began, TV was still playing catch up with a stew of telly pantomimes, circuses, cartoons, Jesus and on the BBC – still represented by just the one channel - the rag bag of comedy and music that was "Christmas Night with the Stars"[7]. There was space for just one picture on the Beeb that night – the 1937 adaptation of Anthony Hope's **"The Prisoner of Zenda"** (7:15pm) starring David Niven and Ronald Colman. Frequently adapted, this was the fourth version for the big screen and would later be remade largely shot for shot as a colour production in 1952. Allowing it onto TV was highly controversial with cinema chains at the time who made their living from rerunning classic movies leading to many declaring a ban on producer David O. Selznick's catalogue for years to come. That would be followed by a play entitled "Tuppence in the Gods" which I'll be honest sounds a lot muckier than it probably was.

Over on the commercial channel, there wasn't even so much as a sniff of celluloid with the big shows of the day being the "Armchair Theatre" play "The Great Gold Bullion Robbery", variety series "The Tommy Steele Show" and "Alice Through the Looking Box" a telly-themed pantomime featuring everyone big on the small screen at the time including Spike Milligan, Dora Bryan, Ronnie Corbett rather typecast as "Dormouse", Fanny Cradock, Barbera Kelly and the collected Bernards Breslaw and Braden.

---

[7] See the chapter "That Thing You Like But Ten Minutes Longer" for more details on that.

1961

A bit of schoolboy whimsy for the BBC with another frequently adapted book character in **"Just William's Luck"** (5:15pm) from 1947 directed by a genuine titan of post-war British cinema Val Guest who gave the screen everything from "Carry On Admiral" and "The Quatermass Xperiment" to "Confessions of A Window Cleaner" and even parts of the original comedic "Casino Royale" from 1967.

Bizarrely, the sequel to "Just William's Luck" from 1948 - **"William Goes to Town"** (5:15pm) – would appear on ATV in the Midlands at the same time thanks to a quirk of the ITV regions at the time. Most of the country also had the option of **"The Pickwick Papers"** (10:05pm) from 1952 continuing the long association with Dickens and Christmas. By that point however, the BBC were already 65 minutes in to the first showing of Hitchcock's 1940 take on Daphne du Maurier's gothic thriller **"Rebecca"**, also produced by Selznick. With "Psycho" not that long out of movie theatres, it was the perfect time to remind viewers of Hitchcock at the height of his powers and it no doubt sent many a viewer checking the locks extra carefully before bed that night.

1962

Another technicolour big hitter for the BBC in the evening with the 1951's **"The African Queen"** starring Bogart and Hepburn at 8:50pm. And one barely a decade old too! Weirdly, due to a deal struck with the London ITV franchise Associated Rediffusion to share costs on film rights, most of the country had already had it in their regions the year prior. As for the third button themselves there was another Dickens adaptation, also coincidentally from 1951, as the now beloved Alastair Sim-starring **"Scrooge"** popped up in a surprisingly late slot past 11pm. Unless you lived in anywhere that wasn't London, the South East or Wales in which case you could've gotten anything from Boris Karloff in **"Colonel March Investigates"** to the 1953 comedy **"Innocents in Paris"** also featuring a cast headed by Alastair Sim. Or if you were in the Anglia region, the news and weather followed by closedown. No manners but what a critic.

1963

No big film from ITV this year although the Dickens connection remained with "Mr Pickwick", a play by Stanley Young based unsurprisingly on "The Pickwick Papers" with the title character played by Arthur Lowe who at that point would be best known to audiences as Leonard Swindley in "Coronation Street", a character who would become so popular he'd be spun off into his own sitcom "Pardon the Expression" and its follow up "Turn Out the Lights". Viewers in the Granada region (which back then also took in Yorkshire and the North West) got a bonus tremble before bedtime though with the 1949 thriller **"The Interrupted Journey"** (10:40pm) With no huge cinematic rival, it was left to the BBC to clean up on Christmas night with one of the very greatest comedies up to that point – Charlie Chaplin's **"The Gold Rush"** (9:25pm) – which brought in over 20 million viewers and quickly got a repeat as the first film on the new-fangled second channel the following April[8]. Over the coming decades, many would associate Christmas week with the appearance of more Chaplin films being broadcast in increasingly dry-mouthed pre-breakfast slots.

1964

And we welcome BBC Two to the mix where it would grow to host many of the more interesting films seen over the festive period. Its first Christmas on air brought viewers two films – the 1939 Bob Hope horror comedy **"The Cat and the Canary"** (6pm) and 1951 musical standard **"Kiss Me Kate"** (8:45pm) which would take some beating by the other networks? And did they? Well, not on the parent channel certainly where they stuck to the business of light entertainment with the evening made up of a Brian Rix farce and an episode of "The Great War", a 26-part documentary series about the first World War. And not even a new one but a repeat from the previous August! It had been a huge hit for the channel and lay the path for a number of similarly behemoth historical documentary series. Fans of historical wars could also enjoy ITV's big film of the evening – the heavily cannon-based Napoleonic era Cary Grant epic **"The Pride and the Passion"** (8pm) from 1957 – which would become the first Christmas Day movie to appear in every region of the country after years of opt outs and alternative programming. One thing that would become synonymous

---

[8] Originally made in 1925, Chaplin had re-edited the work in 1941 to add music, narration and tighter edits. Despite owning the rights to the former the BBC apparently contacted Chaplin himself to get permission to show the later edit – his naturally preferred choice.

with the commercial broadcaster's handling of films, particularly in the 80s and 90s, was on display here – a break an hour in for the news and weather. Whether they also dubbed Sophia Loren to say "Funk you, you Muddy Funster" as she mowed down a crack dealer is sadly lost to the ages.

1965

A film before midday? Have the BBC been ruined by this post-Beatle Britain we now lived in? Appearing at 9:45am were two men who'd later turn up on the cover of "Sgt Pepper's Lonely Hearts Club Band" – Laurel and Hardy - in one of their most beloved full-length films 1937's **"Way Out West"** which was no doubt influenced by the huge ratings Chaplin had got a few years prior. This would also influence **"When Comedy Was King"** (6:30pm) on BBC Two, a compilation of highlights from the silent film era. Also making another appearance on the Beeb was Bob Hope as part of **"Road to Bali"** (8pm), his sixth "Road To…" film with Bing Crosby and Dorothy Lamour from 1952. After a year without a film this was placed right at the heart of BBC One's Christmas Day plans between "The Ken Dodd Show" and…um, "The Black and White Minstrels". Plus, some series called "Doctor Who".

After all coming together in 1964, ITV split the nation again with its choice of viewing including Dickens drama **"The Life and Adventures of Nicholas Nickleby"**, society drama **"The Barefoot Contessa"**, horse-based drama **"National Velvet"** or dick-based drama **"Moby Dick"** *(surely giant whale drama? – Ed)* appearing wherever you lived in the country. The one thing they did all share however was the movie slot coming immediately after The Queen's message which would become a standard practice for many years later.

1966

More multi-region ridiculousness on channel three - at the very precise 3:07pm! - with Audrey Hepburn's romantic comedy **"Sabrina Fair"**, classic John Wayne western **"Rio Bravo"** and a swashbuckling Gregory Peck as **"Captain Horatio Hornblower, R.N."** just three of the six (six!) possible films to slip out after her Majesty had spoken her peace. And the same again would happen in the evening as regions showed an equal number of alternatives although fans of Frank Sinatra could find him simultaneously doing some swinging crimes in the original 1960 **"Oceans 11"** or singing times with Doris Day in 1954's **"Young at Heart"** depending on where your aerial pointed. John Wayne did the business for BBC One in **"The Comancheros"** from 1961 which brought some of the channel's biggest ratings for the day at 8:45pm.

For BBC Two it was comedy all the way with Will Hay's 1937 train based comic classic **"Oh Mr Porter!"** at 4pm and that Bob Hope again as – naturally - the barber of King Louis XV of France in the 1946 comic adventure **"Monsieur Beaucaire"** which closed out the night at 11:30pm.

1967

And here's the man nobody called Marion Morrison again snuggled comfortably in behind Ken Dodd at 9:40pm on BBC One with 1962's **"The Man Who Shot Liberty Valance"** although more excitement was found on the sister channel as the first ever colour broadcast of a film on the big day could be enjoyed thanks to BBC2 switching to colour transmissions that July. The 1950 comedy **"Doctor in Love"** (5pm) was the lucky recipient of that honour before **"The Flute and the Arrow"** (7:20pm), a 1957 documentary about the Muria people of India by Swedish director Arne Sucksdorff. Not being the biggest knowledge in this area, I consulted the Svesk Film Database which states*: "Sucksdorff skilfully mixed ethnographic film with a fictional reality. The film hovered between the game and documentary genre and combined everyday realism with a strong fascination for the mythical, mysterious and inexplicable."* So probably no custard pie fights then. Gotcha.

And ITV? Well, they went bonkers again with no rhyme or reason to the schedules from town to town. Most common seems to have been David Lean's magnificent version of **"Great Expectations"** (8pm) from 1946. Because we all like a good Dickens at Christmas it seems. Even John Wayne.

1968

Finally, ITV manages to get some sort of order as the film at 12:30pm **"Tarzan's Savage Fury"** and the 1951 female-fronted Western curio **"Westward the Women"** (8pm) were available at the same time to all of the UK no matter where they were. As long as they weren't in Ulster. 1946 family guff **"The Courage of Lassie"** at 5pm was not so fortunate though only making it to London as many of the country's provincial franchises – including the brand-new Yorkshire Television – found something more interesting to do. Like watching **"Lords of the Forest: Masters of the Congo Jungle"** airing at the same time on BBC Two, showing life in the - as it was - Belgian Congo. That was followed almost immediately by an obscure take from 1963 on the Camelot tale with **"Lancelot and Guinevere"** at 6:40pm. Bafflingly late at 11:40pm the 1945 MGM musical **"Anchors Aweigh"** which was welcomed by fans of sailors, singing and animated dancing mice. The biggest draw was once again on BBC One with the delightful 1959 comedy **"Some Like It Hot"** making its first Christmas week appearance at 9:45pm but certainly far from the last.

1969

Here comes the Wayne again, **"McLintock!"** in my head like a memory… After a year away from Westerns, BBC One were back in the John Wayne game with this comic action film at 9:15pm, although the once-familiar sight of Ken Dodd beforehand was now taken instead by some chaps named Eric and Ernie. Only one full-length feature film for BBC Two also with most of its schedule taken up by documentaries and music leaving the 11:16pm (precisely) showing of early Peter O'Toole crime vehicle **"The Day They Robbed the Bank of England"** from 1960 for night owls who didn't fancy the Tony Bennett concert on the other side. Another reoccurring face during many of the sixties' big Christmas films returned on ITV at almost the same time of "McLintock!" leading to a rare clash as Frank Sinatra's 1964 Rat Pack comedy **"Robin and the 7 Hoods"** (9:30pm) added a twenties gangster twist to, as you'd probably already guessed, the Robin Hood legend. Yorkshire TV had other plans however, instead scheduling as their big festive night film **"Donovan's Reef"** an 1963 adventure comedy starring… um, John Wayne.

Pop Is Quite Top

With December not only being home to Christmas but – you heard it here first – the end of the year, the last week of each year would often be crammed with retrospectives of the previous twelve months in film, sport, news and, thanks to the traditional hour of "Top of The Pops" before The Queen, pop music allowing a whole nation to come together as one and hear the year's greatest selling sounds before saying "What's this rubbish? Music was better in my day. When's Cradle of Filth on?" etc.

Things feel very different now with our YouTube, Tik Tok and 5G Microsoft-powered injection arms meaning we can watch music wherever, whenever without need for wincing at disgraced disc jockeys recalling earlier chart hits and this chapter will be looking at the progression, rise and fall of pop on TV outside TOTP. With channels taking full advantage of the looser Christmas schedules to play full concerts, opera, ballet and music documentaries there's plenty to choose from and definitely not just because the arts stuff was being shoved out to fill a public service remit quickly at a time most people were watching the other side.

It's definitely interesting to chart the rise of these long-haired beat groups from parent-bothering novelty to a regular part of British society. And none more so than the biggest of the bunch: John, Paul, George and ~~Michael Angelis~~ Ringo. There's always been something oddly Christmassy about The Beatles. It could be their four seasonal number ones or the terrific festive fan club discs they made with folks like Kenny Everett[9]. It could also be down to **"Magical Mystery Tour"**

---

[9] Even their pioneering regular studio producer George Martin got his own Christmas show called "With a Little Help from My Friends" on ITV in 1969 starring some of his collaborators including

making its divisive TV début on Boxing Day 1967 (8:35pm, BBC One). Listed by the Radio Times simply as "The Beatles", this would famously be the first thing critics found to bash the ever-growing group over when expecting a proper film and instead getting the Fab Four farting about for two weeks in September on a bus full of their mates and funny people with no real script having an amazing time and occasionally singing some excellent new songs. An indulgence to many but there's a real exuberance captured in the film which manages to reflect not only the old Britain of coach journeys and strip clubs but also the changes in pop as it got heavier, louder and stranger.

Much of the dazzle was lost by the black and white showing too with its colour repeat on BBC Two not happening until the following week by which time all the critics knives had been plunged. It wouldn't get another repeat until Two's **"The Beatles at Christmas"** season in 1979 which offered fans a rare chance to see not just "A Hard Day's Night" and "Help!"[10] but lesser seen stuff such as the long impossible to find "Let It Be" and the 50-minute quasi-documentary **"The Beatles at Shea Stadium"** (5:30pm, BBC Two, December 23rd 1979) containing footage from their 1965 New York stadium concert on front of 55,000 screaming fans at the height of Beatlemania. First shown on BBC One in March 1966, the material was heavily over-dubbed and partly re-recorded for film due to the sound issues in the stadium, something not properly confessed to until the release of Ron

---

The Hollies, Lulu, Blue Mink and on hand to run through "Octopus' Garden", ~~Michael Angelis~~ Ringo Starr.
[10] Which had premiered in relatively early slots on BBC One during December 28th 1970 and Boxing Day 1972 respectively.

Howard's excellent "The Beatles: Eight Days a Week – The Touring Years" in 2016. Shea Stadium was eventually closed in 2008 after two final concerts by New York native Billy Joel who was fittingly joined at the end by special guest...~~Michael Angelis~~ Paul McCartney.

Following in their footsteps if not their long-term appeal, there were also imports like **"The Monkees"** which hung around for much longer than their chart career survived. The first episode of the prefab four's sitcom would appear here on New Year's Eve 1966 just five months after its US début and featured a typically daft high concept plot ("The Monkees rescue Princess Bettina, Duchess of Harmonica from her evil uncle Archduke Otto") alongside some of the best pop music of the whole sixties, with "Take a Giant Step" the highlight of this first episode. It clearly had an effect on its target audience; within three weeks "I'm a Believer" would reach No. 1 staying there for four weeks, during which time follow-up single "Last Train to Clarksville" entered the chart. Four more big hits would follow in 1967 and the TV show remained part of BBC One's Saturday night line-up for most of the year.

Despite all this mop-topped madness, pop was still very much considered a bit of an oddity by BBC One and ITV at the turn of the decade with it confined usually to a light entertainment format like those hosted by Cilla, Lulu, Cliff and other people with only one name. Luckily a new corner of television was opening up by the mid-seventies with the birth of the Saturday morning magazine show with the BBC's **"Multi-Coloured Swap Shop"** which would regularly feature music in its "Swap Of The Pops" feature[11] or regionally produced programmes such as **"Lyn's Look-In"** (11.45am, ITV, 23rd December, 1978) with Tyne Tees favourite Lyn Spencer and her two sidekicks Malcolm Gerrie and Alastair Pirrie, both of whom would go on to be involved in pretty much every major commercial music series of the next two decades. But everywhere else things had got a little grown up and safe, especially at Christmas time.

BBC Two would happily commission musically related things like **"I Gotta Shoe"** (7:50pm, 24th December 1966), an American Deep South jazz take on Cinderella written by Caryl Brahms and Ned Sherrin with Cleo Laine heading the cast or a rock musical version of The Wooden Horse of Troy legend entitled "**Great Big Groovy Horse**" (7.55pm, BBC Two, December 25th 1975) starring Bernard Cribbins, former Manfred Mann-man Paul Jones, Patricia Hodge, Julie Covington and a pre-"Rentaghost" Michael Staniforth with music by Jonathan Cohen, beloved to the under-fives for his work on BBC children's series "Play School" and it's more mischievous weekend spin-off "Play Away". They'd even stick the rock musical **"Orion"** at 1:45pm on Boxing Day afternoon in 1976 so everyone could enjoy a sci-fi "Noah's Ark in Space" with a book by none other than Melvyn Bragg. But pop music was for the kids, surely? And Two had its post-pub chinstroke for connoisseurs of quality rock "The Old Grey Whistle Test" anyway.

So, what sort of pop artist could break that cycle while still appealing to the pipe-smoking jumpermen of old? How about

---

[11] Many of these performances would be repeated as part of seasonal compilations with Christmas Eve 1977 featuring the disparate likes of Leo Swayer, Tina Charles and Harry Secombe!

Kate Bush and her simply titled 45-minute special **"Kate"** (8:15pm, BBC Two, December 28th 1979)? With two albums already released, Kate Bush was a ridiculously young 21 when she recorded this strange but captivating special which gave the singer chance to experiment with the performance side of her already fairly theatrical act. Indeed, fans didn't know that in May 1979 she'd already performed her last full gig for over 35 years. Bush previewed several new songs in this special despite her third LP 'Never for Ever" not being released until the following September[12].

With the pop chart cork thoroughly out of the bottle now, BBC Two programmed a follow up to Kate for the following year. And that special was um... **"Showaddywaddyshow"** (7:40pm, BBC Two, 30th December 1980) which offered a chance to hear one of the biggest pop acts in the country... just as the hits began to completely dry up. The 'waddywaddy had racked up fifteen top ten hits between 1974 and 1979 but their 1980 album "Bright Lights" had flopped hard as would all of its singles. Luckily a great reception was guaranteed from the BBC Birmingham audience due to it being largely made up of members of the band's fan-club.

Clearly it was time for a change and snotty young upstart Channel 4's **"The Tube"** had its own ideas of how to present music on the television as its 105-minute mix of live music, pop videos and filmed reports went live every Friday teatime, including a special on Christmas Eve 1982 (5:15pm). It was wobbly and awkward and frequently had the piss taken

---

[12] "Kate" would be followed the same night by a "Not the Nine O'clock News" compilation preceding their savage parody of her "England My Leotard" which this special almost certainly partly inspired.

out of it – but was it actually that bad? This festive edition began with some 50s throwback pop with cabaret act Bouncing Czechs, there's a Billie Holliday cover by Alison Moyet, Motown tributes Sylvia and the Sapphires, a youthful Depeche Mode and headlining are electro pop's very own Imagination. Brian Johnson from ACDC also shows up simply because he lives nearby. Outside the UK's hardest man The Hard ("felt nowt!") arrives in a festively decorated tank as resident poet Mark Miwurdz does his mile-a-minute mix of prose and stand up which has a fresh, observational aspect not too common at the time.

Eight weeks in, the presenters are settling into it and Jools Holland takes great pleasure in chasing the audience round. A very pregnant Paula Yates tries to suppress her boredom interviewing several women who once met The Beatles and, on location, Gary Numan talking about his new hair transplant. As a whole, it's not something you'd perhaps want to sit through twice but for that date in 1982, it was unquestionably exciting, current telly and a rare series aimed at young people that young people actually might want to watch. Especially when compared to one of Channel 4's other commissions that Christmas: **"Get Knighted"** (7.15pm, January 1st 1983) featuring comedy pop band The Barron Knights. Duke D'Mond and his bunch of pals had been an acquired taste since they first hit the UK charts in 1964 with their reworded medleys of popular hits of the time. After an initial spurt of success, a "barren" (pun intended) period followed until 1978's "Live in Trouble" single would return them to the top 10 (example lyric: "You Make Me Feel Like Dancing" becomes "My Tailor Took My Pants In".) Their second wind in the charts was starting to peter out by the time of this programme which featured some of their live act and music videos for more recent tracks. It'd be popular enough for a second show the year after called **"Twice Knightly"** (6:15pm, Channel 4, December 25th 1983) and yet again in 1984 when 5.65 million people tuned in for the less punning **"The Barron Knights Show"** (8:30pm, Channel 4, December 28th 1984). The band are still touring today with one whole original member – Peter "Peanut" Langford.

Another unique special from the fourth button was 1985's **"Sunshine Christmas"** (7:30pm, December 23rd) in which excitable TV cook Rustie Lee fronted a *"party for the stars of the black community, held at Kisses Nightspot in South London."* The Peckham club Kisses was home at the time to a residency by the DJ Gordon Mac who decided to form a pirate radio station to play the dance and hip hop that wasn't being touched by the mainstream FM. Tying in with the nightclub's name, this new station would be known as Kiss FM and go legit from early 1990, eventually becoming one of Britain's biggest radio stations.

It was nice to see Channel 4 supporting all types of music in its infancy and never more so than with **"The Chart Show"**. Before it became the dependable bridge between Saturday morning kids shows and Saint and Greavsie talking about the Endsleigh League as if it was important, "The Chart Show" had been devised in 1986 to fill the Channel 4 schedule on Friday tea-times when "The Tube" was on holiday and made an immediate impact thanks to its impressive video recorder-inspired computer graphics and lack of host. It was also the only place that you could ever hope to see a snippet of your indie, dance or rock favourites in an era long before genre specific music channels.

"The Chart Show Christmas Special" would add end of the year spurious awards to the mix with both 'Best Video' (including "Sledgehammer", "True Faith" and Siouxsie and the Banshees' "Peek-A-Boo") and 'Worst Video' included, the latter which was won by Shakin' Stevens, Anita Dobson and even Frankie Goes to Hollywood for their disastrous comeback single "Rage Hard".

With a modern look, a tongue in cheek sense of humour and no presenter egos to worry about its easy to see why ITV wanted it as part of its own line-up. They'd certainly taken their time to place much pop music on Christmas Day with **"The King's Singers at Nostell Priory"** in 1981, Andy Williams in 1982 and **"Jimmy Tarbuck's Christmas All Stars"** with Shaky again in 1983. He'd also crop up singing a bland cover of "Blue Christmas" on **"Pop Goes Christmas"** (5:15pm, ITV, Deccember 26th 1982), an odd mix of current popstars singing seasonal songs with "a sneak preview of some of the hits we can expect in 1983."

Best of the bunch is Dexy's Midnight Runners stomping through a nicely folky "Merry Christmas Everyone" built around Helen O'Hara's familiar violin and added harmonies although Mari Wilson comes close with her 'Wilsations' on a slightly rockabilly take on "Santa Claus Is Coming to Town". There's also a fun electro pop take on "Step into Christmas" by the short-lived Toto Coelo featuring a sample of their own hit single "I Eat Cannibals" on the chorus. And you can probably work out what Musical Youth's "Rudi the Red Nosed Reindeer" sounds like. An edited half hour version of the special would air the following year with a third of the acts snipped out - proof if needed that the world of pop is a fickle mistress. Still, it's a fun way to waste an hour that should've been a yearly thing for decades later – All Saints do The Waitresses, Jona Lewie reimagined by Dizzee Rascal, Rick Astley does The Smiths. Ok, may not…

It was coming quickly apparent that the older style of light entertainment was starting to appear long in the tooth thanks to the boom in video clips that soon came to dominate the decade. We may not have had MTV yet in the UK but we did have the says-on-the-tin presentation titled **"Top Pop Videos 1984"** which cheekily appeared just 45 minutes before the Christmas Day standard "Top of the Pops" on the other side. Pop videos was in such a high demand they even repeated it the subsequent year with an added celebrity host. Unfortunately, it was Jim Davidson with the cleverly titled **"Jim Davidson's Top Pop Videos of '85"** (1pm).

Controversy abounded in 1986 when ITV decide to not only schedule a music show for Christmas but air it directly against "Top of The Pops" at 2pm. Dropping the videos of previous years, **"Ark Royal – The Rock Show"** had Paul Young, Alison Moyet, Bob Geldof, Cyndi Lauper, The Pretenders and Go West… on a boat playing for "a capacity audience of servicemen, their families and Gibraltarians". Whether this barbarity in the face of BBC pop royalty was the reason 1987 contained not a scrap of pop music outside of **"Christmas Family Worship"** is anyone's guess

The commercial network would take one final stab at a TOTP spoiler in 1988 with the excellent **"The Great British Pop Machine"** presented by French and Saunders, one of the great double acts who took the opportunity to mock trendy teen show presenting styles whilst linking performances by the big turns of '88 which, looking back, wasn't much of a halcyon year for the charts with the top ten best sellers of the year featuring three covers of 1960s songs courtesy of Wet Wet Wet, Tiffany and Phil Collins and one outright re-released song from 1969 (The Hollies' "He Ain't Heavy, He's My Brother".) Thank Baby Jesus that somebody invented the Pet Shop Boys...

To give ITV their due though they did commission **"There's Something Wrong in Paradise"** (10pm, December 22nd 1984) - a two-hour adventure set around the music of Kid Creole and The Coconuts, one of the biggest chart acts of recent years. Unfortunately, even with the terrific Pauline Black from The Selecter, The Three Degrees and Oscar-nominee Karen Black, the whole thing is a bit flat due in part to being framed like an old Hollywood musical but confined to the studio and produced on ugly looking videotape. Creole himself - or August Darnell to his mam – is fine as a leading man but the surprisingly serious script by Mustapha Matura with its central theme of racial unrest and guerrilla uprising doesn't quite gel with the upbeat funky 80s pop of the Coconuts. This tough subject matter might explain the surprisingly late 10pm timeslot which will have excluded many of the band's younger fans. AND we still never learned who Annie's daddy was!

Musicals on a telly budget can often be tricky to pull off. An earlier ITV musical extravaganza **"Rock Nativity"** (6.25pm, 26th December 1976) attempted to use the traditional Sunday "God slot" associated with lightly religious programming such as "Highway" to present the Jesus boy birth through the power of ROCK! Music was supplied by former husband and wife power team Tony Hatch and Jackie Trent, the people behind some of the best loved theme tunes in British history. "Rock Nativity" was a rare nationwide production for

Scottish network STV and captured the musical after a nationwide tour.

Slightly more subtle in its occasional dips into religious respectability was **"A Song for Christmas"** a short-lived yearly nationwide contest on BBC One for schools across the country to write and perform an entirely original festive composition on TV in front of a panel containing pop mega-stars. In 1986, this included Bucks Fizz' new girl Shelley Preston, the unmatchable Mike Batt plus chairman Peter Skellern. The winning song in question was "A Child of Peace" from a school in Rhydyfelin, Wales beating into second place the sax-drenched power ballad named "Let's Pray for Christmas" sung by a 15- year-old named Gary Barlow, four years away from being the one nobody liked much in Take That. It's a clip that appeared on a lot of shows after Barlow hit stardom but for all his admittedly comical snood-wearing earnest pretentiousness, the song shows his genuine song-writing talent at a strikingly early age. The whole story was recounted for a brilliant Radio Wales documentary in 2014 suitably titled "Take That Gary Barlow!", which is very worth tracking down. After paying your tax anyway…

Both of those projects underlined how important music was in getting religious messages across on television, even if it was open to ridicule. **"Christian Rave Special"** (12:30pm, Channel 4, December 25th 1995) or "God in The House" as it was billed on screen tried a different approach with a smart waistcoat-wearing young man named Adam Buxton introduced viewers to three different kinds of "religious raves" starting with the Christian dance act World Wide Message Tribe playing in a real church in Cheadle. The songs all sound like contemporary dance of the time with breakbeats and repetitive lyrics, only now with a holy feel. It's pretty much all music (one number is a bit of a sexy slow jam but you know... about Jesus) with pauses for teens to talk about Christ. With up to 500 in the pews, it was clearly finding the audience it aimed at and a peep at Discogs shows quite a number of major label releases for The Tribe including a minor hit on the Billboard dance charts. Next, he pops over to a youth church service in a Bournemouth nightclub called Bliss. This is more hip-hop and praise with a proper full band – even if the talks by leader Johnny Sertin are a bit school-like with the young types sat cross-legged around him. Finally, we're taken to "the Late Late Service" at Woodlands Methodist Church in Glasgow which definitely seems the most fun with lots of dancing and singing plus big video screens. Oh, and candles. Lots and lots of candles.

The YouTube upload I saw of this says "must be a spoof?" It isn't - but it's definitely difficult to tell which side producers World of Wonder were on. It's a hard balance to get right as **"To Hell with the Devil"** (8pm, Channel 4, December 24th 1989) found when following Christian metal quartet Stryper whose quotes like *"Christ was totally cool. He just walked around and caused mass hysteria so he was like the ultimate rock star..."* and *"There's not a Christian B Flat and a secular B Flat. There's just a B Flat..."* are earnest but equally hard not to snigger at from a secular perspective. Glam metal was still all the rage at the end of the eighties with its message of "sex, drugs and more drugs and sex please" only falling down on the whole 'actually listenable music' aspect so Stryper's 1986 album "To Hell with The Devil" stuck a chord with many looking for something different in the sea of hairspray and leopard print spandex, going on to rack up one million sales.

A whispered letter from a 'saved' 15-year-old fan at the start wobbles the line between reality and parody but an interview with a recently bereaved mother who tells of the comfort she gets from the band is suitably moving. Despite the musical clips though, this is a documentary more interested in the Christian part rather than the rock — which can grate after a while as the band and their fans defend their beliefs for the hundredth time despite no negative voices being included, not even those of their contemporary secular groups. There are parallels with the straight edge movement in punk with its "no drink or drugs" doctrine and I suspect a lot of kids featured in this documentary moved over to that scene when twiddly guitar metal started to get stale. But for those keeping the faith Stryper are still very much an active concern and their thirteenth studio album "Even the Devil Believes" reached 92 in the Billboard chart back in September 2020. Praise B (Flat)!

By the end of the eighties, with pop videos no longer a novelty and the cancellation of "Whistle Test", "The Tube", short-lived TOTP-rival "The Roxy" and most of the traditional teatime kids shows that featured chart acts ("Cheggers Plays Pop", "Razzmatazz", "Crackerjack" etc.) now gone, pop on TV seemed to mainly exist on Saturday mornings. Music programmes had been allowed to grow up and diversify like the indie showcase "Snub", the ridiculous explosion of taste that was "The Word" and the much missed "Dance Energy" which embraced hip hop and dance culture at a time when few other outlets knew how. The excitement of the eighties had definitely become a more detached shrug in the nineties. What British pop music needed was a focus, maybe the phrase "British pop" needed to be filed down, to be truncated for the hard of thinking, to become…. Britpop!

The scene, however dreaded to some, had first been mooted on an infamous April 1993 cover of Select magazine declaring "Yanks go home!" in reaction to the wave of grunge-influenced music that had come to overshadow everything alternative since Nirvana's breakthrough in 1991. The Auteurs, Saint Etienne and the hugely underrated Denim were mentioned in despatches but it was Brett Anderson from Suede who dominated the cover. Reflecting this, Channel 4 followed the band on tour for **"Opening Shot: Suede"** (7:30pm, December 31st 1993) ever shadowed by their devoted teenage fans for whom the poppy yet idiosyncratic Suede were clearly made. The perfect crossover band with the tight trousers and big choruses of pop but the mystique and danger of indie which was at a really curious junction where the fanzines, Beechwood Music compilations and charity shop chic had not yet given way to Britpop and bulging big label wallets.

It's also a notable place to check in with Suede who don't yet seem jaded with fame as lead singer Brett Anderson talks to everyone and chatting openly about being a teenage Crass fan. With what was going to come in 1994 its intriguing to note one moment where several fans swarm Anderson simultaneously blanking guitarist Bernard Butler stood right next to him. Few could've predicted how big the scene would get and when it exploded in 1995, the band who rose to the top of most people's affections were Pulp.

The documentary **"No Sleep till Sheffield: Pulp Go Public"** (6.45pm, BBC Two, December 18th 1995) found a band – and in particular frontman Jarvis Cocker – still struggling to take it all in. Interviewed in a full suit on a rumpled hotel bed befitting the seedy yet suburban lyrics the band had become known for, Jarvis is charm incarnate talking about writing songs from the perspective of his thirty-two years with an almost surprised tone when presented with his new screaming teenage fans. He's definitely a kindly older brother figure even of most of these new supporters don't wish to see it that way. Clips of Cocker as a personality on various TV programmes show a path not taken by the indisputably funny and personable lead singer. *"I now have an opportunity to make a lot of money,"* says Cocker contemplatively, *"I could present some game show and turn into Tarby 2: This Time Its Personal. There's a great deal of potential for me to become the saddest person of 1996."*

Not quite seeing Cocker as a sex symbol are his mum and grandma hilariously arguing that they prefer Steve McQueen (*"unfortunately he was very small…"*) and Ronald Colman respectively. Sheffield residents will get a kick out of seeing the city frozen in time as Jarvis eulogises his home at the end of the tour. *"The fashions have moved on but the mentality remains"* he says before playing "Mis-Shapes", a song that still sounds a clarion call to every indie kid no matter how old they are. It's all in stark contrast to the money and attention being thrown at British guitar bands in the two years since the Suede documentary and it all feels like a wonderful dream for the group. Much like Suede though the shine was about to come off leading Pulp to retreat before releasing the dark and brooding masterpiece "This Is Hardcore" in 1998.

Retrospectives of the era now hold aloft the likes of Pulp, Oasis and Blur as the sound of summer 1995 and yet one duo easily outsold the alternative crowd <u>and</u> the pop juggernauts that year with two of the three biggest selling singles plus the top selling album to boot. And all they did it with some of the dullest cover versions ever recorded by human mouths. Step forward Robson Green and Jerome Flynn.

Best known as actors in the popular army drama "Soldier Soldier" (1990-97) the duo had been required to sing "Unchained Melody" in character to fill for a no-show wedding turn as part of a plotline. Viewers in their thousands apparently contacted ITV to find out how to buy this non-existent recording which gave professional snake-oil salesman Simon Cowell the idea to get the pair to sing both that and, to tie in with the forthcoming VE Day anniversary celebrations and soak up those World War II nostalgia quids, "The White Cliffs of Dover". It would stay at Number One for seven weeks. And six months later they'd do it again as the "I Believe"/ "Up on the Roof" double A-side stayed at the top for a month, holding "Wonderwall" in second place to the chagrin of many a parka-hooded indie fan.

To remind people where they'd originally come from, ITV quickly put together the **"Robson and Jerome Christmas Special"** (7:30pm, December 25th 1995) although sadly it wasn't the glorious light entertainment shiny floor spectacular it could've been with the pair stepping out of a giant R and J before duetting with Barbara Dickson. It's more like a slightly more middle-aged version of the BBC teen music magazine "The O Zone" with the chart-topping mates generally pottering about and chatting about their admittedly ridiculous year. Despite hating them and what they'd done to my beloved top 40 at the time, it's hard to argue with the power of television here which created a perfectly-targeted, elderly relative seeking missile of inoffensive pop. It would of course become the key weapon in chart sales the following decade with the rise of reality TV, once again overseen by the Svengali of shite, Simon Cowell.

He wouldn't be the only Simon with plans for world musical domination though as 1996 would be hit out of nowhere by a ten-legged spangly atom bomb of pure enthusiasm called the Spice Girls, all overseen by their manager Simon Fuller. No band could come close to their power or draw during that era and ITV were quick to jump on the Spice Train with **"Spice Up Your Christmas"** (4:45pm, December 25th 1997) a recording of a live gig in Istanbul bookended by the five-piece checking in from a fittingly OTT living room dressed with gifts, candles and a big tree. Sadly, there's only room for four on the sofa so poor Melanie Chisolm has to sit on the floor. When asked what they love about the Christmas period Emma Bunton talks in sickeningly cute detail about kids opening gifts while Mel B just loves the parties. Victoria just wants quality time in Britain (which is presumably why she buggered off to Los Angeles at the first opportunity), Mel C talks about the homeless and unfortunate, and Geri plugs their surprisingly decent new film "Spice World: The Movie" which just so happens to be released the following day. By the relatively short time the film took to come to TV, it had all gone a bit wrong and, from the comfort of the 2020s and televising of the pop sausage machine – ironically started by Simon Fuller and his "Pop Idol" format before being taken even further by Cowell's "The X Factor" – it's easy to see how pop bands are formed, manipulated and exploited especially after the explosion of acts that came in the wake of the Spice Girls' proving how much of a taste for pure POP! people had that needed feeding.

One such act looked like they might be up to the job, scoring six top ten hits in eight months including four number ones. They were a breath of fresh air in their denim with singles like the insanely catchy "C'est La Vie" in May 1998 and its follow up "Rollercoaster", even breaking through into the American top ten. Therefore, it's a shame that when the **"B*Witched Christmas Special"** (9:50am, ITV, December 20th 1999) appeared twins Edele and Keavy Lynch, Lindsay Armaou and Sinéad O'Carroll aired just as their new single had limped in at 13 pretty much ending their chart career.

Using a Star Test-style "confessional" with the girls selecting on screen questions in what we're meant to assume are their very own real-life bedrooms, it's plain to see the four are utterly exhausted and plastering on a grin for both the cameras and host Josie D'Arby. This is most evident when they're asked to watch their videography and can't help noting all the horrible things about making them, like being stuck in a harness for 17 hours *("You won't be making Supergirl the Sequel then!"* says a clearly non-plussed D'Arby.) And this is stuff they've done barely a year prior. None of it seems fun. Despite being clearly ready for a long nap, the four-piece are still funny and self-effacing, the world always needs pop stars with personality. Thankfully after a long break the band are back with a new podcast fittingly titled "Starting Over With B*witched" and all seem to be happy with their place in the pop landscape.

Some ex-popstars of course manage to escape the clutches of music altogether and move into telly presenting. It's a risky move though as **"Ant and Dec's Geordie Christmas"** (5:50pm, Channel 4, December 22nd 1997) found with the teen actors turned popstars turned presenters that also did a bit of pop music trying to find their niche after the end of the underrated sketch show "Ant and Dec Unzipped". This is the naughtier, more laddish version of the duo (*"Goodwill to all men? Does that mean we can still throw snowballs at lasses then?"*) that they'd refine throughout their ITV work but it's a really exuberant funny half hour that both shine in. Recorded "as live" from a cruise boat on the Tyne and featuring the spectacular Kenickie as a house band, it's like "TFI Friday" hosted by a teenage Reeves and Mortimer with a blend of daft sketches, interviews and Evans-like stunts follow such as flinging a giant pie over the River Tyne to Gateshead and seeing what Joe Pasquale sounds like on helium. A few bits are very much of their time such as a video of a boozy womanising Geordie Santa on the 'toon with the duo, former model Jo Guest reading cracker jokes and an aggressive Northern take on the Tamagotchi but items like the pair reading out "bad things to have on your Christmas cards" (including tanks, bums, cheese and dogs 'cementing their relationship') are a lot of fun and feel very much like they'd go onto to do the following year[13].

Regrettably it would not be the next step Ant and Dec were hoping for and after parting ways with both Channel 4 and their record company, maybe they might look into that Saturday morning TV show after all. But don't forget – ITS GOT TO RHYME!!!!!!!

---

[13] Writers Gary Howe, Richard Preddy and Dean Wilkinson would follow them over to "SM:TV" to great success.

The Ballad of Noel Edmonds

"No one in this house watches the telly until the Queen's speech!"

"But it's Noel's Christmas Family Video Accidents!"

(Bottom – "Holy" 29th October, 1992)

It's hard to say when Noel Edmonds became permanently associated with Christmas Day for British people of a certain age…it certainly didn't hurt to have a name that appears in two thirds of all carols. Never afraid to stick his tidy beard out wherever an opportunity presented, Noel began on the wireless and quickly rose up the ranks becoming, aged just 24, the second host of the prestigious Radio 1 Breakfast Show after Tony Blackburn. "Top of the Pops" quickly followed and alongside Blackburn would make his first Christmas appearance on the series in 1973 introducing the likes of Slade, Peters and Lee, 10cc, and A Redacted Sex Offender. Noel would return on the big day in 1975, 1977 and finally 1978 – the latter of which would end up being a severely reduced show due to a BBC strike that December and was simply Noel in a sad looking office set linking into clips from the year.

He'd only return to the Pops one more time after that as his TV work had suddenly taken off in a big way after his kids' call-in series "Z-Shed" was expanded into a Saturday morning magazine series entitled the "Multi-Coloured Swap Shop" in October 1976 which would quickly set the format for pretty much every Saturday morning magazine show that followed with its mix of phone-ins, star guests, cartoons and competitions. In fact, the only part of the show that didn't translate to following Saturday morning formats was the "swapping" aspect itself where children were encouraged to phone in and exchange their unwanted items for other kids' unwanted items or take their old gumph to one of the show's massive outside broadcasts, frequently coming live from a field in the middle of nowhere with an enthusiastic Keith Chegwin.

Despite being a lovable older brother type to millions of kids Edmonds struggled to find that vehicle that would transfer him to proper big people's telly with "Hobby Horses", "Noel Edmonds' Lucky Numbers" and a revival of "Juke Box Jury" quickly coming and going. This would be the bit in the biopic where Noel would look sad for a bit then gets the brilliant idea to take all the best bits from "Swap Shop" and putting it out live on a Saturday night. And consequently, BBC One in September 1982 introduced "The Late, Late Breakfast Show" beginning his Saturday evening reign.

Viewers to those early shows probably wouldn't have imagined that with presenters and features being dropped following a wobbly start but the series would develop into an enormous success over four years with many of Noel's trademark bits like hidden camera surprises, bantering with the audience and big stunts originating there. Rewarding his success, the BBC handed over 90 minutes of Christmas Day 1984 to **"The Noel Edmonds Live Live Christmas Breakfast Show"** a hugely ambitious programme presented from the top of British Telecom Tower with viewer phone ins, pranks, videos, competitions (one prize being the worryingly named "Telecom goodie sack") and lots of outside broadcasts including the much-missed fellow DJ Mike Smith out in the "hollycopter". After adding yet another successful series to his bearded brand with the family quiz **"Telly Addicts"**, Noel and the team would raise the stakes for

1985's show which stretched to a behemoth 125 minutes and featured the *"world's first computer draw"* plus the launch of new charity called Comic Relief[14]. Its perhaps best remembered however for a popular blooper where *"the world's first in-flight pop performance"* sees an unfortunate Feargal Sharkey unable to hear anything at 2500ft throughout a mimed performance of his single "You Little Thief" watched by a helpless Gary Davies and The Krankies.

The tragic death of Michael Lush - a member of the public who was the unfortunate victim of a bungee cord accident when rehearsing for a big stunt on the fifth series of "The Late Late Breakfast Show" - brought the programme to an immediate end in November 1986. As such, it was perhaps a surprise for some to see Noel again barely five weeks later on the swiftly renamed **"Christmas Morning with Noel"** (11am, BBC One) The fact the show went on was no doubt due to the sheer amount of work that would have gone into setting up satellite links around the world including Australia where it was airing live. These efforts resulted in a duet between Cliff Richard and Elton John both on different continents that is as memorable as it sounds. Plus, Mike Smith was looking for Santa in Lapland, how can you miss that?

The final show from the top of the Tower would follow in 1987 at the slightly earlier time of 9am due to the show going

---

14 This involved a lot of short filmed sketches of comics trying to tell jokes to tough crowds with Rowan Atkinson trying to raise a smile from BBC One Controller Michael Grade, Lenny Henry doing "I'm not saying my wife is..." jokes to his then-wife Dawn French and Rik and Ade in Dangerous Brothers mode trying to entertain *"a deaf Chinese mountain ant in a matchbox"*.

out live in more countries with New Zealand, Singapore and Gibraltar now joining Australia for across the sea family link ups[15]. With each special previous feeling more and more elaborate the final edition in 1988 was something of a let-down as the show was cut back to just over an hour and came from Studio 3 of BBC TV Centre just 600 or so feet below the previous location. By this point the dust had settled enough for Edmonds to return to the Saturday night schedule in September 1988 with his "Saturday Roadshow", a fun premise that always insisted it was being broadcast from a remote location despite clearly being a BBC studio set. Feature-wise, it was much the same as his earlier live show with pranks, games, celebrities and comedy bits.

The following year saw Edmonds back on Christmas Day but with a switch to the pre-recorded **"Noel's Christmas Presents"** (11am, BBC One, December 25th 1989), a sentimental but amiable series making wishes come true for those who didn't even know they were wishing them. And they didn't have to meet Jimmy Savile so bonus. For all the stick he gets for being a bit odd, Noel is genuinely great with the public in these early shows. And the presents given out mean the world to the people involved whether it's a new bike for a helpful brother from his sick sister or reuniting long-lost family. The format would be a big part of the BBC's Christmas line-up for a decade with a revival for Sky in 2007 lasting a further six years.

Despite this success, Edmonds hadn't quite finished with live television yet and penance made after the Lush incident both him and the BBC were ready to try again. Carrying over many

---

[15] Noel would pop up again at a more traditional 11:45am for another 45 minutes of live TV after a nice slab of Jesus.

of the best loved features from his previous two series, "Noel's House Party" would go on to be his biggest success of them all. Starting in September 1991, this was Noel in his element as the supposed owner of a stately pile called Crinkley Bottom that was always being invaded by famous folk on a Saturday night.

With "Christmas Presents" filling the bearded quota for the big day itself, the House Party only once flung its doors open during the festive period[16] – **"Noel's Christmas House Party"** on Boxing Day 1992 - perhaps its grandest era, helped but not yet ruined by a certain pink spotted creature that would come to dominate the following year. Mr Blobby had originally been designed as a fake kids TV character to prank unsuspecting celebrities in the "Gotcha" section before becoming a genuine kids TV favourite. It's hard not to join in the excitement as Noel breathlessly rushes through features like "Wait till I Get You Home", "Grab a Grand" and the still hugely exciting and different hidden live camera segment "NTV" although an anecdote by the 'victim' in this specific episode about putting the wrong false teeth in a corpse is a bit extreme for tea-time telly.

Perhaps because it's a live show on Boxing night the celebrity guests are an underwhelming bunch with Joe Longthorne holding a perplexed dog during his frankly exhausting act, Pat Coombs as a dotty organist, some blokes off "The Bill" knocking on the door and Frank Thornton popping up for a daft gag right at the end. Frank Bruno and Nigel Benn are also in the house as part of a public phone vote in for which of them deserves a good gunging (with over seventy thousand

---

[16]   There was a "New Year's Eve House Party" two years later but only because New Year fell on a Saturday.

people ringing in to slime Bruno.) And then there's Tony Blackburn, twenty years on from hosting the Pops with Noel and that episode's "Gotcha" recipient, who is taken in by a fake pink-smock wearing, nettle soup eating "religious group"[17] He's a great sport and comes across sincere and charming as people learned when he became King of the Jungle a decade later.

A genuine unexpected treat - and I don't mean Noel's garish waistcoat - "Noel's House Party" was a mix of sketch show, game show, children's programme and hidden camera series that shouldn't have hung together and yet did for nearly a decade despite him trying out a number of now largely forgotten follow up shows like "Noel Addicts", "Noel's Telly Years" and the bizarre FrankenNoel's Monster one-off that was "**Noel's....And the Winner Is**" (7pm, BBC One December 21st 1996) which took the form of a fake black-tie awards ceremony for lots of daft real hobbies and competitions such as a Gut Barging Contest, a Lithuanian Kissing Marathon, the Toe Wrestling Championships in Derbyshire and Rear of the Year[18]. There are also strange sketches (Noel talks via comically delayed satellite link to "Pricilla Precious live from Hollywood"), star guests (the awful John McCririck, Louise "Not Yet Redknapp" Nurding and depressingly "Kermit the Frog" which turns out to be a

---

[17] Comedy fans will also be pleased that one of the actors in the scene is a young Rebecca Front was appearing in the radio version of "Knowing Me Knowing You" as this went out.

[18] That year's victor was Coronation Street's Tracy Shaw who would be the last solo winner. A man would be chosen too from the following year with Melinda Messenger and... Gary Barlow(!?) the first joint winners. Yay feminism?

green sock puppet being voiced by Bobby Davro) and even a quiz - "Noel's Know All of 96" - with celebrity guests Rhona Cameron, Eddie "I Don't Do Television" Izzard and Carol Vorderman answering questions on the year gone by and mentally composing how to fire their agents throughout.

It's easy to see why Noel was probably looking for something else to host around this point with "House Party" now five years in and seen as a bit naff post-Mr Blobby backlash but this was not to be it. Ill-advised makeovers on both that and "Telly Addicts" quickly hastened their demise. By the time Crinkley Bottom closed its doors in 1999, television was a very different place to when Noel first appeared on it in the early seventies. Regardless of what we've since learned of him being a bit of an oddball, Noel was always a cheery, personable frontman of these shows who seemed to be genuinely enjoying himself and it was great to feel the BBC was this exciting alive 'being' watching over the world, offering company, and setting out its stall as the channel to stick with all day.

Noel would be slung back into the wilderness, going a bit bonkers in the process, before a game show about opening random boxes would put him back in the spotlight again five years later. Merry Blobmas!

So Much Drama

Christmas and drama go together as well as Your Uncle Ken and "unrepeatable options about foreign people". There's a reason so many programmes have been based around what happens when people clash during Jesus' birthday and soaps, admittedly not what they used to be in terms of blockbuster ratings, are still a huge part of the Christmas Day TV landscape. Who can honestly say they haven't seen out the 25th without seeing a punch up in the Rovers Return or an Ebola-filled bomb going off in an orphanage as Phil Mitchell does that face that he does?

Personally, I think **"Coronation Street"** will never top its trick from December 25th 1991. Beginning at the rather unusual Christmas Day time of 2:50pm aka 'just before The Queen', the characters Alf and Audrey Roberts were featured sitting down to watch 'er Majesty whose speech then played out it full before the action continued. And what action it was! Well, alright not compared to the usual terrorist hijackings and murders of present soaps but definitely some filth as Mike Baldwin pops round unexpectedly to her ex-partner Alma's house for a chat and maybe.... a shag? At this point, her character was in relationship with Mike's eternal nemesis Ken Barlow who is clueless to the rampant rumpo taking place across the road.

There's also room for a bit of comedy as constant losers in life Curly and Reg decide to nip into their own supermarket after hours for some supplies - caviar and champagne is mentioned but the ALDI-esque Bettabuy might be more likely equipped with peanuts and a bottle of bleach - before the latter gets his collar felt by the fuzz. Sadly, we're denied the opportunity of Alf Roberts commenting on the Bond film scheduled after or "The Truman Show"-style possibility of him turning on ITV and seeing himself staring back on the screen. Needless to say, **"EastEnders"** fans may have felt a bit ripped off as the soap had tried a similar trick when BBC One decided to risk a new episode of its insanely popular series at 11:30pm on New Year's Eve 1987 instead of the traditional chat show or variety spectacular with the massed Queen Vic regulars tuning into the TV which cut into the real live bonging of the Big Ben bells as 1988 began before returning to Albert Square. Cue a pub piano sing-along of "Auld Lang Syne" and Michelle telling her mum she's pregnant just ahead of the 'duff duffers' of the end theme.

1988 was also the year of EastEnders' first spin-off – the World War 2 set **"Civvy Street"** (7:20pm, BBC One, December 26th) which had been hugely hyped at the time and is now strangely forgotten. "Civvy Street", which inadvertently took the same tack as the same year's "First of the Summer Wine" with the current cast's older characters such as Lou Beale, Ethel Skinner and even Reg Cox, who was found dead in the very first episode, in their prime as younger people. Despite a script by the original series' co-creator Tony Holland, the special only brought in an audience of seven million which was some way behind the parent soap's ratings of 19.1 million and 21.1 million for that same week. The idea was quietly dropped thereafter and the series didn't try another spin-off for over a decade...

The producers of "Emmerdale Farm" would no doubt have loved those ratings in its earlier days. Forever a bit of a punch line, ITV didn't even include it in its Christmas schedules for over two decades thanks to years of random timeslots on whichever of the regions chose to show it since the soap first began in 1972. Drastic action was clearly required and in 1989 the rural Yorkshire soap went under an operation to have the "Farm" part of its title removed. A new production team would expand the focus of the series to the nearby village and then just for good value on December 30th 1993 dropped a plane on it - not a turn of phrase but a real, actual plane - allowing them to completely reshape the series at the same time as getting the attention of audiences who had previously dismissed it (fairly) as a boring countryside affair. The plan worked and **"Christmas in Emmerdale"** (7pm, ITV, December 26th 1995) would be the soap's first ever appearance as part of the big Christmas line up where viewers were treated to not only an inter-pub tug-of-war competition but a cameo from Hunter from waning sports entertainment show "Gladiators". Since 1997, "Emmerdale" has been part of the Christmas Day schedule every year and has so far managed five marriages, three murders, two births and one mineshaft trapping amongst the wacky adventures that happened over the holiday period thus bringing them firmly into line with their fellow woebegone soap operas.

Of course, it wasn't always this way. Soaps were rarely a part of the Christmas Day plan until the 1980s, especially if the programme's regular day didn't coincide with the 25th. Instead, television was the home to regular plays such as **"The Man Who Liked Christmas"** (9pm, ITV, December 22nd 1955) by Canadian playwright Reuben Ship. This had been part of ITV's long-running "London Playhouse"[19]. A huge coup came with the casting of David Kossoff in the lead

---

[19] The network had launched just four months earlier on the 22nd September 1955 in the capital but wouldn't get dedicated transmitters elsewhere in the UK until the following year at which point "London Playhouse" became "Television Playhouse" then "ITV Playhouse" running on and off until the early 1980s.

role. He had won the 1954 BAFTA for Most Promising Newcomer to Film, although is perhaps now better known for appearing in early sitcom "The Larkins" over six series from 1958 to 1964. Sadly, the play is thought long gone as much of this era of television is. As such we're extremely lucky to have Jonathan Miller's adaptation of **"Alice in Wonderland"** (9:05pm, BBC One, December 28th 1966) available on shiny disc.

Fantastically well-made for someone who had never previously directed a film, Miller uses many of Lewis Carroll's original text to create a strange cloudy world between reality and fantasy, with a world of colour filmed entirely in black and white on gorgeous 35mm – a rarity for TV at the time which more commonly used 16mm film – and soundtracked by the hypnotic sitar of Ravi Shankar. Newcomer Anne-Marie Mallik can grate at times playing Alice as the always questioning awkward teenager who has seen it all and is impressed by nothing but she's aided by a cast full of brilliant names mixing darlings of the satire boom (John Bird and his former "Beyond the Fringe" colleagues Alan Bennett and Peter Cook playing Mouse and a brilliantly befuddled Mad Hatter respectively) and the old school (Wilfrid Brambell as the White Rabbit with John Gielgud, Michael Gough and Leo McKern.) Even Peter Sellers crops up for a small role as the put-upon King of Hearts.

Nothing like the famous Disney 1951 version or thankfully the rotten 2010 Tim Burton one, this is a world tinged with fearful tones, preposterous characters and free thinking which builds to a wild and scary conclusion which seems much more in line with Carroll's vision, even if it's not quite the most festive of programming choices.

Alan Bennett would have to wait a few more years before his own first televised single play however despite his success with the sketch show "On the Margin". Originally written in 1969 under the title "There and Back to See How Far It Is", **"A Day Out"** (10pm, BBC Two, December 24th 1972) was worth the wait. A gentle story about Yorkshire cyclists heading out of Halifax to the ruins of Fountains Abbey with the 1911 period detail beautifully filmed in black and white by a 30-year-old Stephen Frears who would return three years later to direct **"Three Men in a Boat"** (7:50pm, BBC Two, December 31st 1975) An all-star adaptation of Jerome K Jerome's timeless tale with a script adapted by Tom Stoppard and Tim Curry, Stephen Moore and Michael Palin as the titular fellows pottering up the Thames with Montmorency the dog. Palin wrote about the experience fondly in his essential collection of diaries "The Python Years" which also contains his attempt to watch it go out live with a house full of New Year guests including children *"a long way from the sitting still and shutting up age"* making it difficult to hear as *"Stephen has opted for a very gently paced, softly played treatment which seems to be at least ten decibels quieter than any other TV shows."*[20]

Unlike now where CGI and video effects are expected in everything from "Scooby Doo" to the "Antiques Roadshow", conveying a sense of wonder through the medium of TV was often a tough one to get right – especially on a BBC budget - and usually left to productions aimed at younger viewers. Few

---

[20] The following week BBC Two would broadcast Palin and Terry Jones's savage take-off of old-fashioned literary "boys' school" adventures "Tomkinson's Schooldays" which would become the first episode of the terrific "Ripping Yarns".

did it better than 1984's stunning **"The Box of Delights"** (5:35pm, BBC One) which came to a conclusion on Christmas Eve that year. Despite being produced as a play for radio many times, John Masefield's 1935 story was thought unfilmable for many years with sequences featuring characters escaping into moving paintings or being miniaturised by the titular box but the full might of the BBC's design, costume and visual effects departments came together with the latest technology available at the time. While these have understandably dated somewhat in the previous four decades due to their reliance on green screen and Chroma key, they still have a charm all of their own that suits the fantastical storyline and helped along by a well-chosen cast including the wonderful Patrick Troughton as mysterious Cole Hawlings who has a secret that accidentally drags a young man and his friends into adventure. Its legacy is so dependable that several people I know still watch their DVD on the original dates it went out on in 1984, using it almost as a televisual advent calendar.

Prior to this, the most infamous non-Time Lord related children's drama for visual effects was probably the haunting **"Pinocchio"** (5:20pm, BBC One) which came to an end on Christmas Eve 1978. A world away from Disney, this adaptation of Carlo Collodi's dark fairy tale in which a naughty marionette is hung from a tree and killed still lives on in many minds of the young viewers who saw it at the time. This was mostly down to the dead-eyed and oft-screeching puppet who interacted with real human actors thanks to the best in-house effects available at the time. It was just one of many excellent children's book adaptations that the BBC produced from series to one-offs like 1980's mysterious **"The Bells of Astercote"** (4:40pm, BBC One, December 23rd) based on Penelope Lively's 1970 novel "Astercote". When their dog runs off into the woods, two children meet the simple yet clearly haunted chap Goacher who talks of a mystical chalice and the Black Death. The awfully posh acting children along with the common archetypes of the tale's small minded country folk mean it's hard not to snigger a little at lines like *"I'm sure we all agree that that was a most interesting chat by the Vicar on the subject of brass rubbing…"* but when the secret of the wood finally come to light, the story shifts gears with some exciting 'us vs. them' village at war oddness that echoes the conflict in earlier BBC children's serial "The Changes".

"Ghost in the Water" (4:40pm, BBC One, December 31st 1982) would follow with a nicely-paced script by Geoffrey Case adapting Edward Chitham's 1973 book of the same name. Renny Rye would direct, two years before his work on "The Box of Delights", although there's no charming old time schoolboy adventures here as viewers are thrown into a modern scene of two teens exploring a rainy graveyard which we learn via flashback is for a school project. It's a brilliant hour of telly with the supernatural segments and eerie dream sequences superbly rendered with a deliberate blue-tinted Hammer Horror style look. No cringing at rotten child acting here and the school-room scenes are believably awkward for the time even if the broad, authentic Black Country accents are authentic but may put you in mind of Vic and Bob's "Slade at Home" sketches. It was a far cry from those ruddy hooligans at **"Grange Hill"** (5:20pm, BBC One, December 28th 1981) who got a rare Christmas special out of uniform at the school disco. The episode's storyline had been suggested by 16-year-old Paul Manning, the winner of a "Blue Peter" competition earlier in the year. Paul also got to appear in the episode too as one of Grange Hill's rival schoolboys from Brookdale boys try to nick the disco gear. There's also a shattered Tucker missing the bus because he's so tired from watching late night videos with his brother who works at "an electrical 'olesalers". (*"He brought some 'ome…whatsits name? Er…Saturday Night Fever… Alien", "The X version?" "Yeah, that's very stupid innit? They won't let you in the flicks to see it but you can buy it on video. It's crazy!"*)

It was the sort of harder edged kids' drama that Children's ITV was producing a lot of themselves throughout the eighties with series like **"Dodger, Bonzo and the Rest"** (4:15pm, ITV, December 22nd 1986) about a large mixed foster home in London. The Christmas episode doesn't pull its punches with a domestic violence storyline featuring Phil Daniels as a truly nasty piece of work and a kid trying to reconnect with her alcoholic mother. A little levity is offered when Tony Slattery turns up as an exasperated under-manager battling with two homeless revellers (Gordon Kane and Malcolm Rennie). A smart, well-written series that never talked down to its audience and is very much the parent to the later Tracy Beaker and "The Dumping Ground" series long after ITV gave up making much drama for kids.

Indeed, you can't really imagine ITV doing a lot of things they used to, such as their programming for Tuesday 29th December 1981 when viewers were greeted at 9pm by a three and a half hour Trevor Nunn adaptation of Chekov's **"The Three Sisters"** featuring Suzanne Bertish, Roger Rees and Timothy Spall in the cast. Little respite for low culture enthusiasts was found when flicking over to BBC One which was simultaneously showing **"Artemis '81"**, a visually interesting but utterly baffling three-hour science fiction play starring Hywel Bennett and Mr Sting[21] about the battle between good and evil for Mankind's future set on a ferry.

The succeeding year ITV broadcast another adaptation of a popular play although **"Anyone for Denis?"** (8.45pm, ITV, December 28th 1982) couldn't have been any more different. One of many TV projects with a Private Eye connection, "Anyone for Denis?" was a stage farce by John Wells based on his incredibly successful series of spoof letters from the magazine – ostensibly written by Denis Thatcher to friend Bill Deedes, editor of The Daily Telegraph. The original stage production opened to huge acclaim at the Whitehall Theatre in 1981[22] eventually snagging the Thatchers themselves for a charity performance of the show with Margaret telling a reporter through a plastered smile: *"We had a very enjoyable evening. It's a marvellous farce and I do think that the girl who played me, Angela Thorne, she's wonderful. She's obviously spent a tremendous time studying everything I do"*. She was less sure of Wells' bumbling, boozy, slightly bigoted representation of 'im indoors, feeling it was "not at all right".

When compared to what passed for mainstream drama elsewhere in the world at the time, it was like British telly was sealed in a satisfying old school bubble during the mid-eighties. Case in point would be the undeniably brilliantly named "Silent Knight" from the second season of **"Knight Rider"** (4:40pm, ITV, December 27th 1984), a series about a sentient perm (David Hasselhoff) and his sassy car - a Pontiac

---

[21] You know, from the massive house on the estate.

[22] Minus the column's original co-writer Richard Ingrams who sniffily declined to take part fearing the worst.

Firebird Trans Am with artificial intelligence (voiced by William Daniels) Here the pair are set with the task for finding a tuxedo for "the annual Christmas banquet" (insert gif of Harry Hill looking sideways to camera) but are interrupted as a group of naughty men in Santa outfits hold up a bank. When a teenage wise-guy stupidly steals something from them for no reason other than to further the plot, Michael and KITT try and keep him safe and maybe have a crack at his fit older sister into the bargain. Throughout the episode - which has otherwise next to nothing to do with Christmas - there are…let's say complicated depictions of gypsies that probably wouldn't fly today. But a man and his feisty, talking car? Some things will never get old. Indeed, the five or so attempts to reboot the franchise more than prove that. As do the ratings of 2021's biggest new drama hit in the States **"The Equalizer"**, a reimagining of the tough 80s action series starring veteran British actor Edward Woodward. A mix of spy fiction and violent justice (as his newspaper classified advert read: "Got a problem? Odds against you? Call the Equalizer".) that lived in the shadows with a menacing title sequence designed to get into the head of anyone ever thinking of walking alone in the dark. Not the sort of series that did Christmas specials, right? Well…

"Christmas Presence" (9.00pm, ITV, December 22rd 1988) begins reasonably enough in the glorious Winter New York full of lights and ice skating and big decorated trees. It's a nice touch and a reminder of the hope that remains in even the blackest night as the main drive of the story has our titular hero being called on to protect a six-year-old boy with AIDS from drunken, riled-up bar patrons. Using the irrational fear of the Reagan era and ignorance of the still emerging disease, "The Equalizer" manages to raise one of the toughest issues of the time with sensitivity, actual medical facts and a sympathetic central character. And speaking of London geezers who frequently end up on the wrong side of a fist, **"Minder's Christmas Bonus"** (9:45pm, ITV, 26th December 1983) was one of four seasonal specials the exceptionally popular comedy drama received over its fifteen-year run including the feature length "Minder on The Orient Express" in 1985 which not only took pride of place on the Christmas night schedule but also the cover of the prestigious double issue of the TV Times that year.

"Christmas Bonus" would be the only episode of the series however to feature anything to do with the season of goodwill as Terry and Dave the barman putting the Christmas tree up in the Winchester Club as Arthur gets angry phone calls from 'er indoors - which is what we called wives back then before they invented Twitter. If this sounds a bit sleight as a plot, it's merely a wraparound device to shoehorn a load of old clips together from previous shows. Despite this cheapness, there's something quite entertaining about the unlikeliness of the "Minder" characters looking back over four years of comic arguing, elaborate deals and good old-fashioned Cockney punch ups as a warm up for the fourth series beginning in January 1984. Considering she was the subject of a single at No.26[23] in that very week's Top 40, you think the wife would be happier. A nice little earner indeed.

---

[23] The record in question "What Are We Going to Get For 'Er Indoors?" had even been performed by Dennis Waterman and George Cole on "Top of the Pops" the week prior. It would peak the following week at number 21.

Over on Channel 4 the station was still producing drama of all types and moods from "Brookside" to the hugely successful Barbara Taylor Bradford adaptation "A Woman of Substance" and as it entered the nineties was about to hit a particularly golden patch with series such as "GBH", "The Camomile Lawn" and Dennis Potter's "Lipstick on Your Collar". There was still a place for the weird and wonderful though and Malcolm McLaren's extraordinary part-musical history of one of London's most famous places **"The Ghosts of Oxford Street"** (10:05pm, Channel 4, December 25th 1991) definitely fits that bill.

In a worryingly prescient opening, McLaren, mask wearing and miserable, stumbles around in the shadows as jazz music plays and the former Sex Pistols manager opines about the modern world. He decides a Christmas Masquerade ball for the dead is in order at the site of a former ballroom and, before you know it, Alison Limerick is here with a techno theme song to celebrate "magic" being "back". That's about as much plot as is required from this typically high concept piece by the 44-year-old and yet oddly timeless McLaren who monologues about London's darker side and his favourite subject - himself - in amongst appearances from the hippest pop acts of the era with the Happy Mondays covering the Bee Gees' "Staying Alive" dressed as highwaymen being taken to the noose. Later, Tom Jones plays department store magnate Gordon Selfridge and Nasty Nick Cotton (or John Altman if you'd prefer) appears as opium addict Thomas De Quincey haunted by visions of Sinead O'Connor. A gorgeous looking film, directed by McLaren himself with a dreamlike quality, is the sort of thing Channel 4 was brilliant at – a mixture of high and pop culture that doesn't take itself too seriously.

The same could have been said about **"The Bogie Man"** (9:25pm, BBC Two, December 29th 1992) starring Robbie Coltrane as Francis Forbes Clunie, a Scottish mental patient who goes round solving mysteries that are invariably in his own head. Based on a comic strip by Judge Dredd's creator John Wagner with Alan Grant and artist Robin Smith it's a concept that could've been brilliant but sadly doesn't really work. This is partly due to Coltrane not really nailing the madness of the character and partly because the creators were been kept out of the process of converting it to the small screen. This pretty much killed off Francis until 2005 when new story "Return to Casablanca" began in the Judge Dredd Megazine. A shame as few casts could boast Craig Ferguson, Fiona Fullerton AND Midge Ure.

Not even Tim Firth's **"The Flint Street Nativity"** (9:30pm, ITV, December 22nd 1999) managed to snag Ure although it seemed to have every bugger else in it. A brilliantly true to life staging of a first school play, Firth and director Marcus Mortimer got around the whole children shouting in crowns element by casting the cream of the best TV talent. There's Dervla Kirwan as a jealous Gabriel plotting to steal the role of Mary from Josie Lawrence who is more concerned with the "tatty head" of her Joseph (Jason Hughes) who'd probably rather be playing with Frank Skinner's "A Question of Sport"-obsessed Herod or Ralf Little's Star of Bethlehem who is always getting into bother because of 'dares'. Jane Horrocks' shepherd is the over-opinionated know-all of the group *("You're not a proper donkey, you've just got a donkey's 'ead!")* and The Wise Men - a lisping Neil Morrissey, Julia Sawalha and Tony Marshall argue over which has the best present for the new saviour whose head is definitely not going to fall off. It's an incredibly funny well observed play (*"He peed his leg but its ok, I mopped it up wi' a sheep..."*) with the backstage chatter revealing much about the children's home lives. Stephen Tompkinson's narrator wants to learn all of his lines because his dad who "doesn't sleep in their house anymore" is coming and Shamima (Mina Anwar) cries in the toilets because she'll "get done" for not helping her social-climbing family show off to their neighbours. John Thomson's innkeeper is the eternal misunderstood rough lad who not so secretly holds a candle for Mary but Mark Addy's box-headed Donkey is perhaps the most unfortunate of the lot having an 'accident' on stage and struggling to process his grandma's death. (*"Me mum said she were old...but I looked inside her cardigan and she was only 38-40"*)

To complete the illusion of size, high camera angles and giant sets are used with the audience are kept in shadow throughout until the final act where we see they're played by the same actors as the kids. The parents are flawed, struggling and trying to get through adding just a little more realism to the script – a reflection of the commitment it took Tim Firth to gather enough real-life school anecdotes from his family and teacher friends over ten years. Having already created the wonderful comic drama "All Quiet on The Preston Front" for the BBC, Firth was by this time one of the UK's best screenwriters and would go on to script "Calendar Girls", the Madness musical "Our House", "Kinky Boots" and the fantastic "Cruise of the Gods". "The Flint Street Nativity" was never the constantly repeated treasure it should've been but has had more than a successful afterlife in stage adaptations. A wonderful way to spend an hour. Just don't ask who wants to play Mary...

Only Fools and Ratings

How do you find something new to say about "Only Fools and Horses"? It is the programme that, more than any other, the British public have taken to their heart and refused to let go of decades after its initial conclusion. When one of the series' key supporting actors John Challis died in September 2021 the digital channel GOLD quickly scheduled two full days of related "Only Fools…" programming. The fact that the schedule they'd already had planned before his death was 75% Trotter based says much for its enduring appeal.

Much is made of the small audiences "Only Fools" got when it first launched and the late date and timeslot for its initial Christmas special **"Christmas Crackers"** (9:55pm, BBC1, December 28th 1981) shows its standing in the BBC at the time. Its rating of 7.5 million watching seems impressive by today's multi-channel standards but still ten million off the top-rated programme of that week ("Coronation Street" with 17.1m) and even the top-rated sitcom (another slow-burn hit "Last of The Summer Wine" bringing in 16.9m on Christmas Day and with "The Muppet Movie" on the other side too!)

It's a fun episode though albeit one that feels like a string of skits showing how the Trotters spend a typical Christmas Day although it has a secondary purpose as a 'preserved in aspic' time capsule of life in 1981 with Rodney perving over a book about "Body Language", Del mocking him about his activism over American cruise missiles being held in Britain *("You went one and half days on hunger strike then sent out for a curry!", "Well, I was starving!")*, circus shows being on both channels, an argument over what "birds" want, night spots that play "Shakin' All Over" from 1960 and making a mint on "fire salvaged Rubik cubes". It's especially the final scene, set in the tacky Monte Carlo nightclub that feels like an extended sketch rather than anything from the later series but in retrospect it's nice to see three great actors discover the characters as they go, particularly the much-missed Lennard Pearce who gets the lion's share of the best gags here.

Despite the slow start, the BBC committed to a second series plus not one but two appearances that following Christmas with **"Diamonds Are for Heather"** (7:55pm, BBC One, December 30th 1982) showing the sentimental side that would soon become the backbone of the series as Del tries to court a single mother. Much less known and highly sought after by fans for years was "Christmas Trees" a short eight-minute sketch featuring the core cast written especially for **"The Funny Side of Christmas"** (8:05pm, BBC One, December 27th 1982), a Frank Muir-hosted compendium of new pieces from the most popular comedy series on both channels.[24]

It was a good time for Trotters Independent Traders as viewing figures slowly crept up and three weeks before Christmas, the episode "A Touch of Glass" became the first episode of "Only Fools and Horses" to attract a UK television audience of over 10 million. And yes, it's the one with the chandelier. To capitalise, the BBC stuck some repeats out in the summer of 1983 where it finally found a bigger audience leading to a third series and the first special to go out on the 25th December itself. **"Thicker Than Water"** (9:35pm, BBC One) is the first episode of the series to really flesh out the Trotters' history as the brothers' good

---

[24] Also included were rare items from Les Dawson, "The Fall and Rise of Reginald Perrin", "Yes Minister", Smith and Jones, "Last of the Summer Wine", "Three of a Kind", "Butterflies", "Sorry!" and David Jason again in "Open All Hours". A Smith and Jones sketch featured too would lead to them getting their own series in early 1984.

for nothing dad Reg appeared for the first and only time. The episode would be BBC One's fourth most watched programme of Christmas 1983 behind "The Two Ronnies, "All Creatures Great and Small" and the movie "Flash Gordon" setting the pattern of growing success that would come over the decade.

The cast would also pop up in a quick live sketch on Russell Harty's teatime chat show **"Harty"** (6:40pm, BBC One, December 21st 1983) where they try to sneak a free meal from the show's party ("Grandad: *"'Oo's Russell 'arty?"*, Rodney: *"He's like Michael Parkinson but with O levels!"*) before the host himself awkwardly comes over and initiates an improvised conversation that the cast try to do in character despite being referred to by their real names.

There would be no special in 1984 with writer John Sullivan dedicating himself to a feature length episode of his latest series "Just Good Friends" for Christmas Day and the filming of "Only Fools and Horses" series four. Tragically, it was during this period Lennard Pearce fell ill and unexpectedly died leaving a huge hole in the series to be filled partially by Buster Merryfield as Uncle Albert. He at least looked the part when dressed as Father Christmas on the front cover of 1985's double Christmas Radio Times heralding the biggest adventure to date – the 90-minute film **"To Hull and Back"** (7:30pm, BBC One, December 25th 1985).

As a bit of an extra promotion on Christmas Eve of that year the BBC's "Breakfast Time" would send its consumer reporter Lynn Faulds Wood to speak to a rogue trader who had sold a gullible member of the public "White Mice" saying they would turn into horses when midnight struck. The stall holder is of course Del who by now was already a beloved figure in British television. As a character he could've gone badly wrong coming across as boorish, rude and occasionally quite cruel…all of which he unfortunately does in **"A Royal Flush"** (7:05pm, BBC One, December 25th 1986) which is by far the series weakest moment up to that point.

Rodney has met a girl who turns out to have aristocratic routes which Del smells as an opportunity to make some money. It's a simple premise but it doesn't really work due to Del being actively unpleasant to his brother and any chances of being happy. It's not entirely John Sullivan's fault with the episode being commissioned late in the year as he was already at work on the final episode of "Just Good Friends" airing the same day an hour earlier. A series of cast illnesses and schedule clashing - including a detour to perform an in-character sketch as part of that year's "Royal Variety Performance" - meant the final edit would not exist until the early hours of Christmas Day with one possibility mooted that the cast performed the in-studio bits live on the day. Eventually a severely reworked version made it to home release taking around 18 minutes out of the episode and adding in a laughter track missing on the original broadcast.

After this the regular weekly series took a few years' break leaving more time for Sullivan to concentrate on the specials with the extended **"The Frog's Legacy"** (6:25pm, BBC One, December 25th 1987), **"Dates"** (5:05pm, BBC One, December 25th 1988) and **"The Jolly Boys' Outing"** (4:05pm, BBC One, December 25th 1989) all in the series' best loved episodes.

"Rodney Come Home" (5.10pm, BBC One, December 25th 1990) might contain some of the bleakest moments ever broadcast on Christmas Day. The 75-minute programme explored Rodney's failing marriage which had been at the centre of the sixth series in 1989, now extended to 50 minutes per episode allowing for more character development. Thankfully for viewers fearfully wondering what would happen next, series seven started just five days later on 30th December continuing the soap-plot comedy drama style the programme had edging towards for a few years. Elsewhere on One that same day were festive episodes of "Bread" and "Birds of a Feather" along with the usual chuckle-fest "EastEnders" leading to potentially one of the most miserable Christmas Day schedules of all time.

The fairly underwhelming two-part 'mistaken identity' special **"Miami Twice"** as next dominating both Christmas Eve and Christmas Day 1991 although the former comfortably came top with 17.7 million vs. the second instalment's 14.9 million viewers. Though audiences didn't know it at the time, the regular series had come to an end with David Jason, Nicholas Lyndhurst and John Sullivan all being pulled in different directions with projects like "The Piglet Files", "The Darling Buds of May", "Sitting Pretty", "Goodnight Sweetheart" and "A Touch of Frost". The specials **"Mother Nature's Son"** (6:55pm, BBC One, December 25th 1992) and **"Fatal Extraction"** (6:05pm, BBC One, December 25th 1993) would be the only new material for nearly five years though by now the constant cycle of repeat runs had begun, something which will continue on one channel or another until the inevitable heat death of the universe as we know it.

These re-runs kept audiences sated until everyone was ready to return although few probably suspected that the series would have a permanent conclusion. But Christmas 1996 was to see our last trips to Nelson Mandela House with three final shows running across the week – **"Heroes and Villains"** (9pm, December 25th 1996), **"Modern Men"** (8pm, December 27th 1996) and **"Time on Our Hands"** (8pm, December 29th 1996) which nearly 25 million people go out live - no mean feat in the satellite era - making it the fifth most watched TV programme ever.

The trilogy is remembered mostly as the source of Del and Rodney famously dressed as Batman and Robin along with the former passing out when hearing he's finally becoming a millionaire but at its heart is a running thread about Rodney and Cassandra's attempts for a baby which unexpectedly for a mainstream TV sitcom ends in a heart-breaking miscarriage. Taking place in the second episode "Modern Men" after 45 minutes of daftness about Del considering a vasectomy and Rodney looking for work, the news hits like a sucker punch and inspires genuine emotion for these characters that have become so real over the previous fifteen years.

As the third and final part of Sullivan's set of stories begins you can't help wondering how they're going to address this sadness, be it a time jump or just completely ignoring it. For a while, it seems like the latter is going to be the case with Raquel fretting about her parents meeting Del for the first time. The Trotter brothers go to clear out their garage but upon returning find themselves trapped in the grotty lift at Nelson Mandela House. It's here that the episode's real stand out moments occur as a despondent Rodney begins to slowly let go and talk about what happened after bottling it up and drinking it away for weeks. Featuring just David Jason and Nicholas Lyndhurst, this is one of the most powerful scenes from not just any sitcom but TV in general. John Sullivan had already tackled grief beautifully when including the real-life death of Lennard Pearce into the fourth series but here the pain is so real because we as a nation have seen Rodney go from pot-smoking shiftless adolescent to a grown married man. He's part of the family. The Rodney plonker. The speech he gives is truthful but devastatingly performed by Lyndhurst who has never been better.

"Me and Cass were so happy, Del. We were looking forward and all we could see in front of us was a big wide highway and we were just cruising like we were in a Rolls-Royce. And suddenly it came to a shuddering halt - just like the poxy lift... Suddenly 'Happy Families' became 'Dungeons and Dragons'. And I've never felt sodding pain like that in all my life."

After that it's more or less back to the gags as Raquel's dinner party goes naturally awry before her antiques dealer father spots the watch that would make their fortune. After years of saying it, the Trotters were now actually millionaires. Cue a walk into an animated sunset (*"This time next year we could be billionaires!"*) and a genuine celebratory tear for a series that went from just another sitcom to the series that frequently united the nation. Countless documentaries and clip shows followed with David Jason releasing about 400 books "just remembering" that he was originally asked to play Grandad or Mickey Pearce's hat or the chandelier at some point. A thousand "Nag's Head" pubs popped up in every sunny European location full of ex-pats and truckloads of official tie-in merchandise - every bit as tacky as some of the items Del sold on his market stall - appeared in shops all over the country. It ended on a high with an unrealistic situation that everybody wanted to happen.

Everyone went back to their other projects and despite the demands from lunatics who don't understand when something is best left alone, John Sullivan promised he would never write another "Only Fools and Horses" script….

…and then he bloody wrote three. Premiering on Christmas Day 2001 through 2003 this new trilogy felt like a cruel joke which needed to return the Trotters to the bottom of the pile as idiots who blew their own fortune. There didn't seem to be any reason for the series to be back anymore other than the fact people liked the characters. It only got worse with the Boycie-centric spin-off "The Green Green Grass" which felt like an escapee from the 1970s and the sort of broad wacky programme "Only Fools and Horses" had once felt believably different next to. A prequel drama "Rock and Chips" had potential to develop into something interesting but John Sullivan's death in 2011 brought a final full stop to the Trotter family saga.

Naturally, the repeats continued. And the merchandise. Not to mention an official musical co-written by Paul Whitehouse with Sullivan's son Jim and Chas Hodges which opened to huge acclaim in the West End in 2019. It's the series that has come to define and unite the country long after Trotter's Independent Traders ceased trading. Cushty. Or as Del might say: "Bonnet de douche".

That Thing You Like But Ten Minutes Longer

So that's yer Fools and the Horses taken care of but which other sitcoms have become staples of Christmas Day?

Surprisingly it's not many as you think. Unlike a game show or variety special, it's a big risk to give a huge chunk of Christmas real estate to characters from one series. Sid James' post-Hancock series **"Citizen James"** was a big hit of the time and even that had its one Christmas Day episode in 1961 moved back from 7:30pm to 12:20pm.

The BBC got round this potential short-term boredom with the televisual selection box **"Christmas Night with the Stars"** (1958 – 1972) a yearly special featuring lots of shorter new scenes from comedies of the time alongside more standard variety acts. 1964 for example featured Benny Hill, Dick Emery, Billy Cotton and the Barron Knights alongside pieces from Thora Hird in middle aged couple comedy "Meet the Wife" to Richard Briers and Prunella Scales in middle class couple comedy "Marriage Lines" and "The Likely Lads" which had only begun on BBC Two a fortnight earlier. A similar prime time leg up would be given to new series like "Dad's Army" (1968) and "Monty Python's Flying Circus" (1969) in later years.

ITV decided to try / steal (delete as appropriate) the format for themselves with **"All Star Comedy Carnival"** (1969-1973) which as the title suggests jettisoned the non-comic material for bite-sized segments of popular sitcoms like "Please Sir!", Rodney Bewes in "Dear Mother…Love Albert" and "The Lovers" plus snippets from sketch comedies "Cribbins" and "Sez Les" along with the panel game "Joker's Wild". They were a great way to try out shows that might not have the stature to get a full half hour and it's surprising to a degree the format has only been tried again twice the early seventies – once with Fry and Laurie in 1994 introducing items from the big BBC Two comedies of the time and another in 2003 which was really just a standard variety show hosted by Michael Parkinson.

There'd been plenty of variety shows with comic moments from folks like Arthur Haynes, Ken Dodd and Harry Secombe but the first proper situation comedy aired on Christmas night seems to be ITV's **"On the Buses"** in 1970. It's not a series that has aged well with its stilted dialogue, gritty sets and grotesque man-child "heroes" trying to constantly have sex with women a third of their age though many still seem to enjoy it via its worryingly regular repeat runs. That episode "Christmas Duty" (8:30pm), where the two leads are forced to work on Christmas Day, seems to have only made it to the 25th because that was the slot the then present series[25] had already been running in anyway.

After that its back to the circuses, pantomimes and general light entertainment until 1974 when BBC One gives forty minutes over to Michael Crawford's slapstick-heavy sitcom **"Some Mothers Do 'Ave 'Em"** (7:15pm) which clearly went down well enough for the series to get the same treatment on Christmas Day 1975 and 1978. ITV countered with tinsel-topped editions of its new RAF recruit comedy **"Get Some In!"** (7:30pm) and the appalling racial humour of **"Love Thy Neighbour"** (8pm) on Christmas night 1975 with the latter being represented in the TV Times by a cartoon featuring a Gollywog popping out of a Christmas cracker to give you an idea of the general tone there. Despite this subtle humour, the popular Elaine Stritch and Donald Sinden culture clash

---

[25]   Series four with this being the 18th new episode of the sitcom since 1970 began. Strewth etc.

comedy **"Two's Company"** (10:35pm, ITV) would be the only situation comedy to appear in 1976 and despite being a bumper year for telly viewing, the closest 1977 got to a sitcom was "Emu's Christmas Adventure" (4:40pm, ITV) in which Rod Hull's crotch-fanatic bird helped Santa.

After more Frank Spencer in 1978, the Seventies would close with two very different series on Christmas night. On ITV there was **"George and Mildred"** (6:15pm) about a bickering couple struggling to adapt to a middle-class lifestyle spun-off from the equally popular "Man About the House" (1973-96) Sadly, bar a disastrous feature film[26] this would be the last adventure for the bickering Ropers after the sudden death of co-star Yootha Joyce from liver failure aged just 53. It was a blow for everyone, especially ITV who had held the series in such high regard it had even included it in the first night's schedule after an eleven-week union pay strike which wiped all but one region off-air between August and October 1979 for almost the entire UK.

One programme that benefitted hugely from the lack of competition caused by the strike was **"To the Manor Born"**, a gentle series about the butting heads of an upper-class widow and a 'new money' millionaire which peaked at 23.7 million viewers for its finale making it the most watched TV series of the 1970s. As such it was probably a quite easy decision to place it at 8pm between Mike Yarwood and "The Sting" on the last Christmas Day of the decade.

Despite bringing a new decade, 1980 would be a sparse year for the comic genre with a regular episode of "Dallas" taking

---

[26] See the chapter "Hey! A Movie! The Eighties" for more.

up schedule room on the Beeb while ITV squeezed as much as they could out of big signings Morecambe and Wise.

Eventually seen as a naff thing your nan watched, it's easy to forget **"Last of The Summer Wine"** (7:15pm, BBC One, December 25th 1981) was frequently post-watershed and a ratings powerhouse in the eighties and easily the biggest comedy hit of the festive week ahead of "The Two Ronnies", Mike Yarwood and more bloody "Dallas". The best ITV could offer in return was a 11:40pm repeat of "Rising Damp" from 1975…unless you lived in the Ulster region which just decided to close down for the night instead. Compo, Clegg and Foggy would back on Christmas Day 1982 and though the series would run another 28 years, it would be its last placing on the main night with 1983's special broadcast on December 27th. It would however be unique as, before the process became common, this was the first movie length TV episode. Shot entirely on film and presented without a laugh track "Getting Sam Home" was based on creator Roy Clarke's own 1974 novel – simply titled Last of the Summer Wine – mixing some daft slapstick with a genuinely beautiful film about death, sex and the passing of time that might just surprise people who only saw the latter episodes, particularly after Bill Owen's passing. There was a lot more depth than old men in bathtubs perving over stockings and Roy Clarke's writing deserves more praise than it gets for the way it told character-driven stories with real character.

If any programme probably made it look old hat, it was the brash modern new adventures of the Trotter family and, as you may have seen a few pages back, 1983 welcomed **"Only Fools and Horses"** (9:55pm, BBC One) in the first of fourteen appearances on Christmas Day although this is undoubtedly the latest scheduled with later episodes popping up in slots anywhere between ten past three to 9pm.

Despite the Trotters taking the 25th off in 1984 John Sullivan still provided a 90-minute episode of his romantic comedy **"Just Good Friends"** alongside the holiday camp romp **"Hi-de-Hi"** which would rest its white-shorted buttocks in more or less the same slot in 1985 too. It had competition on ITV however from **"Fresh Fields Christmas Special"** (6:45pm), a hugely popular series about a couple left to fend for themselves after their kids leave home that passes more than a glancing similarity to BBC One's "Terry and June". This suburban festive frippery has Julia McKenzie (the manic, easily-flustered Hester) and Anton Rodgers (the dependable William) dealing with neighbours popping in to huge audience applause, the wrong turkey being brought home and flustered spinster secretaries. The clash may have been too much for many viewers and neither series ended up in their respective channel's top ten for the week.

John Sullivan returns with over two hours of Christmas Day 1986 to himself thanks to "Just Good Friends" and "Only Fools and Horses" although neither clash with **"A Duty Free Christmas"** (9pm) on ITV which finds hapless holidaymaker Keith Barron getting into some cuckolding scrapes on a seemingly never-ending vacation. A revival of the popular but controversial "Till Death us Do Part" featuring the opinionated and self-confident Alf Garnett, **"In Sickness and in Health"** feels like a strange series to make a Christmas Day appearance but there it is on 25th December 1987 after more Trotters and even a lunchtime "Porridge" repeat. Similarly, as it's a Friday, **"The Golden Girls"** shows up in its regular Channel Four slot at 10pm although there's not a speck of snow to be seen.

1988 brought more Del Boy and a 75-minute episode of Carla Lane's dreary but massively successful Liverpudlian saga of a thieving family **"Bread"** which would be seen by a staggering 18 million people. Both would be back in 1989 too as would yet another edition of "In Sickness and In Health". By now ITV were seemingly running low on sitcom hits although several clips would appear in 1989's one-off seasonal compilation **"Christmas Comedy Box"** presented by the awful Jim Davidson where anyone deciding against "Crocodile Dundee" on the other side could see rare Christmas Day appearances of Garry Shandling, Rita Rudner and Joan Rivers. It was to be the beginning of the end for the third channel's sitcom attempts as the nineties loomed...even Channel 4 managed to sneak in a repeat of **"Cheers"**!

From 1990 to 1999, ITV would only feature a sitcom on December 25th twice - **"French Fields"** (10pm, 1990), a cross-channel spin-off of the previously mentioned domestic sitcom and the awkward romantic comedy **"Watching"** (6:30pm, 1991) after which the channel concentrated mainly on light entertainment or drama[27]. For BBC One though it was the last great decade for the situation comedy with Christmas Day slots given over to the departing **"Bread"**, the bawdy **"Birds of A Feather"** (four appearances, 1990-94), shameless social climbing in Roy Clarke's **"Keeping Up**

---

[27] They would however schedule two and a half hours of older sitcom specials including "Get Some In", "Rising Damp" and "Watching" again, plus "Nearest and Dearest" and more recent hit "The Upper Hand" between 12:30pm and 3pm on Christmas Day 1992.

Appearances"** (three appearances, 1991, 1994-95), the magnificently dark and brilliant **"One Foot in The Grave"** (three appearances 1994-95, 1997), fluffy Dawn French vehicle **"The Vicar of Dibley"** (two appearances, 1996, 1999), the boisterous flat share adult comedy **"Men Behaving Badly"** (two appearances, 1997-98), Caroline Aherne and Craig Cash's wonderfully realistic **"The Royle Family"** (1999) and indubitably **"Only Fools and Horses"** (five appearances. 1990-96).

"Men Behaving Badly" was particularly of note as many critics noted its script was exceptionally adult for the traditionally more family-focussed Christmas night (especially the 1998 episode which had a subplot about Gary becoming addicted to 'instructional' videos and masturbating too much) as the BBC struggled to find a replacement for its rapidly depleting catalogue of sitcoms. But with new hits like "Ghosts", "The Goes Wrong Show", "Staged", "The Cleaner" and "King Gary" appearing in more recent years maybe one of those will be deemed worthy of calling up to the biggest day of the year soon. Or at the very least Mrs Brown and her Boys get a second joke....

Hey! A Movie! The Seventies

1970

A new decade begins and first out of the gate for both channels were films before The Queen's now fixed 3pm slot, a relatively untested concept but one that would quickly become standard. ITV struck first at 11:35am with yet more regional variations including 1951's **"Tarzan's Peril"** in London, **"Tarzan and The She-Devil"** from 1953 in the Tyne-Tees region and, on Yorkshire, the 1960 comedy **"Sands of the Desert"** featuring Charlie Drake who looks a bit like Tarzan if you squint your eyes really close together. More chaos would ensue after Her Maj with strange 1964 semi-animated Don Knotts talking fish vehicle **"The Incredible Mr. Limpet"** and a rare Bob Monkhouse acting role in 1961's **"Dentist on The Job"** the most notable. In the evening after the 10pm news, the same would happen again with something different in practically every region with HTV almost certainly the winner thanks to their scheduling of **"Breakfast at Tiffany's"**. Just try not to think about Mickey Rooney.

No such nonsense on BBC One who led at 12.35pm with **"The Story of the Silver Skates"** a strange dubbed TV movie based on Mary Mapes Dodge's 1865 novel "Hans Brinker (aka The Silver Skates)" with music and lyrics by the brilliantly named Moose Charlap and featuring future "Confessions Of…" film rogue Robin Askwith in the lead role alongside Doctor Who film urchin Roberta Tovey as his sister Gretel. A mite classier at 9:15pm was more Audrey Hepburn, this time with Cary Grant as part of the slick 1963 thriller **"Charade"**. Helpfully that would finish at 11pm just in time for viewers to flick over to BBC Two for even more

Hollywood royalty as 1953's **"Kiss Me Kate"** got another seasonal run out by the sister channel.

1971

Another Stanley Donen directed thriller – 1966's **"Arabesque"** - would be BBC One's only big contribution in terms of film in 1971. Instead, it was left to the smaller station next door to put in the celluloid leg work with forgotten 1964 Western **"A Distant Trumpet"** and 1957's romantic drama flop **"The Barretts of Wimpole Street"** placed as a double feature from 5:30pm onwards. Confusingly scheduled for 11:20pm was the 'midnight movie' – 1964's **"Marnie"** – which had been Hitchcock's following feature after the more horror-based "The Birds" and "Psycho" and returned him to the psychological thriller format many of his earlier works had been rooted.

And now – deep breath – as we look at what the ITV regions have wrought this time and…bloody hell, they all seem to be showing the same thing! Starting with 1963family fantasy **"Captain Sindbad"** (11:30am) before **"King Solomon's Mines"** from 1950 (3:10pm) in the afternoon and the sprawling but hugely fun 1956 comedy adventure **"Around the World in Eighty Days"** (8:35pm) rounding off the day. The premiere of 1963's **"The Great Escape"** (6:30pm) on the 28th December however would be the most successful film of the whole week although just as exciting for many people was the feature-length edit of the "Doctor Who" story "The Daemons" that was on just before it!

1972

BBC Two would be the first to flash their flicks with a 11:25am broadcast of the odd Harry Nilsson animated musical **"The Point"** which had been made for CBS in the States the previous year. This first version would be unique in that it featured Dustin Hoffman as the narrator but only for one showing after which his contract ran out and he was replaced by various folks over the years including Nilsson's regular drinking buddy and future "Son of Dracula" co-star Ringo Starr.

Although I don't really feature them much in this book as other people have written far more eloquently on the subject[28] Morecambe and Wise were already the cornerstone of BBC One's Christmas TV schedule by this point and their specials would often be the lead in to a big film for BBC One such as the terrific Neil Simon-penned 1967 comedy **"Barefoot in the Park"** (9:15pm) So, who were the stars of ITV's big teatime comedy movie that year? Erm…that would be Morecambe and Wise in their second film **"That Riviera Touch"** (3:10pm) from 1966 when the duo were still regulars on the third channel. It's not especially good but was definitely a counterpoint to BBC Two's only other film of the day – Laurence Oliver's 1944 epic Shakespeare adaptation **"Henry V"** (3:05pm) I'm sure Eric would say he's never even seen the first four…

---

[28] Such as Louis Barfe's 2021 "Sunshine and Laughter: The Story of Morecambe and Wise" which I recommend to anyone with even a passing interest in the duo

1973

More Neil Simon loveliness on BBC One at 8:35pm with Jack Lemmon and Walter Matthau as the original 1968 **"The Odd Couple"** – none of your Thomas Lennons or that one where they were pets, thank you – in the plum slot after Morecambe and Wise. Being that channel's only film of the day, BBC Two went to town with three big hitters that couldn't be more different from each other with 1954 musical staple **"White Christmas"** (11:35am), lusty Thomas Hardy epic **"Far from the Madding Crowd"** (3:15pm) and the big screen Hammer-produced 1967 version of the BBC's own **"Quatermass and the Pit"**[29] (10:30pm) which had first terrified audiences back in 1957 as a six-part serial.

As for ITV, another variation at 11:30am offering heroic dog antics but not the one you're thinking of in **"Lad, A Dog"**, more loin cloth leaping about with **"Tarzan's Greatest Adventure"** and a choice of black and white double act with **"Laurel and Hardy in Toyland"**[30] or **"Abbott and Costello in the Foreign Legion"** depending on where your antenna pointed. 3:10pm was home to strange nun-based fun **"Where Angels Go, Trouble Follows"** from 1968. Later on, Frank Sinatra's back as a prisoner of war with the World War II adventure **"Von Ryan's Express"** (9pm) followed in some regions by an episode of the American sitcom based on a popular 1968 movie called… "The Odd Couple".

---

[29] Frustratingly for fans of creepy tales, an adaptation of M.R. James' dead children-based spookiness "Lost Hearts" would air opposite the final third of the film on BBC One.

[30] A slightly abridged version of "Babes in Toyland" (1934)

1974

After a slow build up over the decade prior, having the biggest feature films was now more than ever a priority for the major channels with three films appearing on both BBC One and ITV throughout the day. The former must have felt pretty pleased with itself when popping Laurel and Hardy's **"Way Out West"** (12:25pm), the much-loved 1969 John Wayne drama **"True Grit"** (4:05pm) and two and a half hours of the Second World War masterpiece **"The Bridge on the River Kwai"** (8:45pm) onto its schedule for the day, especially with Morecambe and Wise taking a rare year off outside of a Parkinson special later in the evening.

ITV weren't going out without a fight though beginning with the Pip and Jane Baker co-written **"Captain Nemo and the Underwater City"** (11:30am) which attempted to make a Civil War era prequel of sorts to Jules Verne's "20,000 Leagues Under the Sea". The same period of history would also be the backdrop for the evening's big draw – 1969's **"The Undefeated"** (7:50pm) which would give viewers a second chance to see John Wayne that day. Between the two **"Those Magnificent Men in Their Flying Machines"** (3:05pm) from 1965 could offer no such setting but did provide a perfect teatime spectacular where I'm led to understand that viewers could see planes that went up, tiddly up, up AND down, tiddly down, down. But don't quote me on that.

BBC Two decided to duck out of the fight mostly with a suitable collection of concerts and documentaries; including one about American stuntman Evel Knievel hosted by the natural choice for such matters – David Frost - but did find room for another showing of **"Henry V"** (6:10pm) and Ronnie Barker's short dialogue-free comedy **"Futtock's End"** (8:45pm) which had been co-produced by David Paradine Productions – that's David Frost to you, sunshine. A fun if not hilarious romp with some of Barker's trademark "knickers knackers knockers" humour in there thanks to several scantily clad ladies. However, if you just want to see the taller Ronnie naked except for strategically placed bubbles this is definitely the film for you!

1975

With BBC One leading with the very first TV showings of **"The Wizard of Oz"** (4:05pm) and **"Butch Cassidy and the Sundance Kid"** (8:45pm) in a schedule already full of hits like "The Generation Game", "Morecambe and Wise" and "Some Mothers Do 'Ave 'Em" you'd be easy to convince that ITV would just give up and not bother that year. Instead, they took the higher road with a bit of culture with Franco Zeffirelli's fun version of Shakespeare's comic play **"The Taming of the Shrew"** (8:30pm) Featuring an all-star cast headed by Elizabeth Taylor and Richard Burton it's the sort of film you'd never expect to see on the ITV of the last thirty years and all the better for it.

Earlier on at 3:05pm was the channel's biggest draw of the day - **"Doctor in Trouble"** - the final big screen adaptation of Richard Gordon's medical comedy books. Considering ITV was already home to a long-running separate sitcom version based in the same fictional St Swithin's hospital and scripted by names like John Cleese, Bill Oddie, Douglas

Adams, Phil Redmond, Jonathan Lynn and actual qualified medical professionals Graham Chapman and Graeme Garden it was perhaps little surprise. The commercial broadcaster's biggest film of the season had been the 1962 epic **"Lawrence of Arabia"** and with its structure already handily broken into two parts in the original full film, it made perfect sense for ITV to split David Lean's groaning three-and-a-half-hour feature over two consecutive nights on the 22nd and 23rd December.

For someone born in the eighties like myself, big old Hollywood blockbuster films seemed fairly commonplace each holiday period but many had been surprisingly quite fresh to TV as the movie studios had regularly returned them to hugely profitable repeat performances in cinemas in those simpler times before home recordings. The concept was so new that only two months before Lawrence aired, on 28th October 1975, "Dr. No" had become the first Bond film to appear on telly. Despite the novelty the film did not rate highly with part one going up against a BBC One premiere of the film **"Born Free"** plus the big hits "Are You Being Served?" and the "Mastermind" final.

1976

Please sir, I wish to see the musical adaptation of **"Oliver"** (4:15pm) on BBC One at as opposed to what's on the other side which is a big screen adaptation of the ITV comedy… erm, **"Please Sir!"** (3:10pm) The big guns - quite literally - would be out in the evening though as the lavish but critically mauled 1970 spectacular **"Waterloo"** (8pm) took up two and a half hours of prime Christmas night with Rod Steiger as

Napoleon Bonaparte squaring up to Christopher Plummer as the Duke of Wellington in front of an estimated 15,000 period dressed extras. Only slightly less bombastic was BBC One's **"Airport"** (8:45pm) which featured an equally all-star cast and pretty much started the trend for disaster movies that we'll see over the coming years that was only stemmed by "Airplane!" proving how ridiculous they were. Jimmy Cagney closed out the night in BBC Two's only film of the day **"Yankee Doodle Dandy"** (11pm) The musical, which won him an Oscar, is one of those many roles Cagney played that seem to be forgotten now outside of him tommy-gunning people in a big hat and saying "you dirty rat". Which he didn't even say in the first place.

1977

The year of bumper ratings and 400 million people and their cat watching Mike Yarwood, Brucie and, for the final time on BBC One, Morecambe and Wise. So where did that leave the films? Amazingly with **"The Wizard of Oz"** (4:05pm) again in almost the same slot it had been in the year before on the BBC. The musical biopic **"Funny Girl"** (10:05pm) starring Barbra Streisand would be the day's only new film which due to the mass of light entertainment to show wouldn't start until 10:05pm. By that point ITV's big film of the night Richard Attenborough's **"Young Winston"** (7:15pm) from 1972 had just concluded after nearly three hours of youthful Churchill based antics. By no means a bad film it had been unfortunate to be fodder against perhaps the strongest Christmas Day line-up of all time. Earlier on the almost totally forgotten **"Robinson Crusoe and the Tiger"** (12pm) in which amazingly Robinson Crusoe washes up on an island which has a tiger on it and newly made British comedy film compilation **"To See Such Fun"** (3:10pm) had done little to stem the tide either. And speaking of water, BBC Two had its own premiere – a domestically much loved 1976 film from Australia entitled **"Storm Boy"** (5:50pm) which would be a rare non-imported hit film in the country. Based on a story by Colin Thiele, a second adaptation would follow in 2019 with Geoffrey Rush and Jai Courtney amongst the cast.

1978

"I love James Bond. Bloody Bond. I bloody love him." Yes, we've finally hit our first James Bond film on Christmas Day after the previous six[31] had slowly crept out to huge viewer figures between October 1975 and September 1978. **"Diamonds Are Forever"** (6:45pm) brought Sean Connery's initial time in the role to a close with a tale of smuggling and, as you'd expect, a giant laser device. Despite beginning a tradition, the film would only do moderately well for ITV in the ratings thanks not only to Yorkshire TV holding it back until a less competitive January timeslot and also an overlap clash with another huge first showing on the other side – **"The Sound of Music"** (4:20pm) As if to prove Yorkshire right, the next Bond film "Live And Let Die" (1973) would instead debut in January 1980 and bring in the series' highest ever viewership with 23.5m, not to mention the highest ratings for any film on television ever. From that point only 1974's "The Man

---

[31] Seven if you include "Casino Royale" in 1973 which would be the only Bond-related film to premiere on the BBC.

with The Golden Gun" in 1980 and 1983's "Thunderball" semi-remake "Never Say Never Again" in 1986 would bow on the 25th.

Outside of Julie Andrews up a mountain, BBC One was on dodgier ground with the first showing of the newly dead Elvis in the dreadful **"Clambake"** (11:35am) from 1967. This was followed at 8:45pm by the disappointing TV sequel to a film they'd shown on Christmas Day four years earlier. **"True Grit, a Further Adventure"** had been produced for America's ABC network in the May of 1978. Replacing John Wayne as Rooster Cogburn was Warren Oates who did at least have some Western credibility after appearing in a number of Sam Peckinpah's bloody, brutal takes on the genre including 1969's "The Wild Bunch" and 1974's "Bring Me the Head of Alfredo Garcia".

And when I say BBC Two showed a two and a quarter hour Russian drama directed by noted Japanese auteur Akira Kurosawa at 4:20pm, you'd either reply "classic BBC Two!" or "Ah yes! **"Dersu Uzala"** from 1975, a classic treatment on Russian explorer Vladimir Arsenyev and his exploration of the Sikhote-Alin region of the Russian Far East over the course of multiple expeditions in the early 20th century!" Three stars. Some funny bits.

1979

It seems appropriate that the decade ends with two of its greatest contributions to the cinema with 1973's comedy crime masterwork **"The Sting"** (8:30pm) and 1972's bittersweet pre-war musical favourite **"Cabaret"** (10:45pm) appearing for the first time on BBC One and Two respectively. ITV still brought a fight however with a repeat showing of **"Goldfinger"** (3:15pm) and ridiculous star adventure vehicle **"The Three Musketeers"** (6:45pm), the former of which went up against an obscure fantasy comedy called **"The Gnome-Mobile"** (4:30pm) from 1967 on BBC One. No doubt gathering dust in a corner of Disney+ in 2021 back then this a bit of history due to being the first full length feature film from the House That Mickey Built ever to be broadcast on Christmas Day after decades of denying the TV rights thanks to profitable cinema re-releases. It's still not very good, mind…

Queen's Greatest Hits

"The Queen. Huge ratings every year but never gets a series!"
– Harry Hill

There are some things that you couldn't imagine not being there as part of the British Christmas Day experience. Paper hats, tolerating relatives, unpleasant sprout related smells... and then there's The Queen, her Majesty of All Britain and That. Born to reign over us so be quiet Jason your nan's trying to listen. Her annual message relaying her thoughts on the previous year has been a long-standing joke for many, dividing the traditionalists from those who could never really understand what was so exciting about some old lady rambling in a mansion.

Wherever your own opinions lay, she has been a staple of Christmas Day since 1957 regular as clockwork at 3pm on BBC One and ITV although the live broadcasts gave way in 1959 presumably so she could watch what was on the other side. Only twice has she missed that regular slot – the first time in 1963 when she decided to go audio only due to being six months pregnant with Prince Edward. The main subject that year was about helping to lessen world hunger and *"the need for humanity to be ambitious for the achievement of what is good and honourable"* which was a bit of a let down after 1962 which was all about going to space and the launch of Telstar.

She also ducked out in 1969 fearing over-exposure after the whole clan had appeared in the Richard Cawston's access-all-areas documentary **"Royal Family"**. Permitted ostensibly to celebrate Charles being made Prince of Wales and following the family over the course of the year, the programme remains one of the most watched broadcasts in the UK with

30 million tuned in on both BBC One and ITV, only beaten by the 1966 World Cup Final and the funeral of a woman who wouldn't join the family for another decade. Without a message, the BBC replayed the 90-minute programme as it would again in 1971, 1972 and 1977 before an edict came down barring it from future broadcast. Outside dodgy video recordings, it remained under lock and key for decades, even being the focus of an episode of Netflix's economically truthful "The Crown", before unexpectedly leaking to YouTube in June 2021.

In the seventies, Her Majesty would juggle motherhood and with trips around the world, her silver wedding anniversary, Princess Anne getting hitched, becoming a grandmother for the first time, the first message recorded out on location (1975) and the first subtitled speech by Ceefax (1979). Sadly, reports that she later challenged Turner the Worm to a fight when losing at Bamboozle could not be confirmed at this time. One event, however, dominated the decade for Elizabeth and that was, of course, the Sex Pistols being denied a number one with "God Save The Queen" due to alleged chart fixing. Sorry, that should've read "the Silver Jubilee" which dominated everything in 1977 to polarising effect. BBC Two had even re-run all seven hours of her 1953 Coronation on New Year's Day that year. One of the earliest surviving TV recordings, it was an intriguing experiment and for those watching on catch-up, Liz was crowned at half-twelve. I wonder if she tuned in for this encore performance? "Oh gawd, look at one's hair!" etc.

Energised perhaps by the effects of the Jubilee, the ratings for her 1980 message were at an all-time high with a peak of 28 million viewers in the UK, all of whom no doubt tuned in to view the 80th birthday knees up celebration of Queen Elizabeth (TV's "Queen Mother") who responded by living for another twenty-two years, only occasionally nearly dying due to some fish. The wedding of Charles and Diana in 1981 would give the nation another day off to recapture that jubilee street party spirit although gun obsessed teenager Marcus Sarjeant clearly wasn't so enamoured firing six blanks from a firing pistol at her during that year's Trooping the Colour ceremony in June. His actions saw him become the first person since 1966 to be prosecuted for Treason. The year afterwards Michael Fagan would famously break into the Queen's bedroom in Buckingham Palace although he seemed more interested in having a potter about than any major criminal intent.

William and Harry came along in 1982 and 1984 respectively, the latter year finding another rare regal documentary on TV – **"The Queen and Her Ceremonial Horses"** (7:15pm, ITV, December 23rd 1984) although this one was a lot less controversial than "Royal Family". Sharing her love of four-legged hay munchers, Liz appears here in a rare chatty mode and it's a genuine pleasure to see her enthused and casually nattering to camera about breeding programmes and training like – gosh – a regular person. Frustratingly this much needed Royal humanity is all buried in one of the dullest things ITV have ever broadcast with endless shots of muttering small men in brown coats trying not to make eye contact with people deemed above their station.

Fittingly now her house was once again full of nippers, her 1986 speech addressed "society's responsibility towards children". Which presumably meant not braying them and that. That film, as the next six would also be, was produced by another documentarian of note - David Attenborough although detailing the mating habits of The Queen were presumably off the table.

The next big evolution would come in 1989 when she read part of her Christmas speech live on stage at the Royal Albert Hall a few days prior to the 25th. This meant for the first time an audience heard part of the speech prior to its international broadcast, all of whom were presumably bootlegging it secretly to sell down Camden Market the following day "as seen on TV…"

Probably the most famous speech in terms of how many references and parodies of it followed was 1992 and her 'annus horribilis' which contrary to popular belief does not translate as 'rotten anus' but 'horrible year'. This was due to a series of events including Windsor Castle catching fire, pizza enthusiast Andrew getting divorced and Fergie's subsequent topless toe-sucking, Princess Anne getting divorced from Mark Phillips, the inevitable divorce of Charles and Diana flamed by the Andrew Morton-penned tell-all book "Diana: Her True Story" and the revelation of "Squidgygate": a series of intimate conversations 'somehow' taped between the princess and her friend James Gilbey.

She nonetheless dusted her fire-damaged crown off raising caution in 1993 when mentioning the "Global Village" we now lived in and the concern we'd soon be dominated by constant "overwhelming" news, a chilling echo of what would come in just a few years with Diana's death leading to the 24-hour news cycles and constant online updates we have today. As well as that dreadful event, 1997 was also the year of her golden wedding anniversary which would be a balancing act for first time producers of the Christmas message ITN who would go onto take turns with the BBC producing the Christmas broadcast from here on, with Sky being added to the rotation in 2017. The fact that the BBC who previously had the monopoly had made that still incredibly controversial tell-all "Panorama" interview with the late Ms. Spencer was definitely nothing to do with the decision. Nope.

This 1997 speech was also the first to go out on the internet so people of the world could revel in the glory of a stuttering 0.5MB Real Media video file that takes 2 days to download. Just what Lady Di would've wanted. Since then, she's seen in more grandchildren, celebrated a Golden AND Diamond Jubilee, attended a couple of weddings, survived a pandemic, lost her husband and broadcast in widescreen, podcast, HD, 4K and even 3D. She was even deep faked by impressionist Debra Stephenson in 2020 in one of Channel 4's "alternative Christmas messages" which have been part of the channel's Christmas Day since 1993.

Going out at the same time as Her Majesty these short films feature voices that had been relevant or had something to say about the year just passed. The first **"The Alternative Queen's Message"** was first launched as part of the channel's "Christmas In New York" strand with the 85-year-old writer, performer and trail-blazing eccentric Quintin Crisp offering opinions on his adopted country and the incumbent President Bill Clinton. Speaking in New York's famous Plaza Hotel he is damning about the idea of a welfare state (*"They watched many episodes of Sesame Street, and they wish for change. They want everyone however poor, however foreign, however idle, to be eligible for health care. The trouble with this grand notion is that it will cost money. A lot of it!"*) although his comments on the opposite sex (*"women have now decided to become people. This is a change for the worst. Women were nicer than people…"*) and the USA itself (*"America is not in a sufficiently secure position to bomb the world, so it has decided to save it, which may prove to be just as expensive, and will certainly take much longer"*) may require a certain amount of tongue in cheek.

The subsequent year's "Black Christmas" theme sought the opinion of the Reverend Jesse Jackson, a figure who had made international news when he stood as a Presidential candidate for the Democrats in 1984 and 1988. He spoke about moving politics and race relations forward, a message that sadly never stops being relevant. This was followed in 1995 by former actress and model Brigitte Bardot in her role as an animal rights activist for "Beastly Christmas" week.

1996 proved how big a difference a year would make as Rory Bremner spoofed Diana, Princess of Wales's post-marriage independence (*"I'm still big, it's the monarchy that has got small."*) with a comic chat show called "The Time, The Palace". It's a timely reminder of how her personal life was anything but with constant press stories and communal fascination of millions the world over. Over on Sky One, a ghoulish half hour "year in review" of her life had just finished. For those who didn't live through 1997 it's impossible to convey the mix of emotions and reactions to Diana's tragic death that year. In his show "Glorious", Eddie Izzard equated it to showing the final episode of "The X Files" unannounced in the middle of the night and people going "oh I was watching that…"

With her now 'The People's Princess' by 1997, a Shankhill teenager called Margaret Gibney spoke about peace in

Northern Ireland which was still several months away from the Good Friday Agreement being finalised. Having already met with Tony Blair and Hillary Clinton that year, the 13-year-old Belfast girl had become famous by writing to over 150 world leaders calling for an end to all wars.

Doreen and Neville Lawrence, the parents of murdered teenager Stephen Lawrence, spoke in 1998 about the need for governments to honour their son's name with stronger laws against racist and hate crimes, yet another message that remains eternal and necessary over twenty years on. After that, it perhaps seems a strange choice to give the slot to Sacha Baron Cohen as "The 11'O Clock Show" character Ali G who had broken through that year despite being from one of the most hateful programmes ever broadcast.

The slot has continued until the present day with names from the world of entertainment (Sharon Osbourne, Adam Hills, a couple from TV's "Wife Swap") with those who had been through era-defining moments including a 9/11 survivor named Genelle Guzman, the former President of Iran Mahmoud Ahmadinejad, government whistle-blower Edward Snowden, survivors of the Grenfell Tower fire and Brendan Cox whose wife MP Jo Cox had been senselessly murdered in 2016. Sadly, perhaps due to channel choice or Channel 4's move into less controversial or ground-breaking television, these rarely have the impact many of them clearly deserve.

Lenny Henry: The True Spirit of Christmas?

When asked to think of the names that most reflect the classic telly Christmases of past, the same folk – The Queen, Morecambe and Wise, Mike Yarwood, David Jason, The Two Ronnies etc. – are understandably constants but rarely does the comedian and actor Lenny Henry get a mention. Yet looking at his list of credits from the previous forty-five years shows how regular he was as a sight on Christmas week.

He'd first pop up sadly as part of **"The Black and White Minstrel Christmas Show"** (8:15pm, BBC One, December 20th 1975), an archaic variety format featuring old timey songs performed by white entertainers in blackface that signed up the sixteen-year-old comic after he'd won the national TV talent contest "New Faces" in some strange move to presumably seem less pointlessly racist. Thankfully for his career and soul "The Fosters" came along shortly after. An LWT sitcom about a modern black family living in London, this was a quietly revolutionary comedy based on the hit US series "Good Times" (CBS, 1974–79). With many British sitcom hits adapted for America in the seventies ("Man About the House" becoming "Three's Company", "Steptoe and Son" remade as "Sanford and Son" etc.), The Fosters was a rare reversal of the trend. The American show had begun as a more serious-minded comedy handling big issues but would soon devolve into a cheap catchphrase-led vehicle for breakout character JJ and his repetitive "Dy-no-mite!" phrase which took the country by storm. Over here in the UK the zaniness was turned down a notch and JJ became loveable layabout Sonny, played by an enthusiastic 17-year-old Lenny.

The plot of **"New Year with the Fosters"** (10:30pm, ITV, January 1st 1977) was taken pretty much wholly from a second season "Good Times" episode titled "The Dinner Party" in which the family suspect an impoverished elderly neighbour (Irene Handl) has made a meatloaf from dog food. Spoilers: she hasn't. The Foster family would return for a second and final series of 13 episodes in April 1977.

When that ended, Lenny graduated to **"TISWAS"** where he got to learn about thinking on his feet as part of a live TV programme and followed the cast to the less successful adult spin-off "OTT" before. His future lay over on the BBC Though and after a Boxing Day 1981 appearance on comic game show **"Blankety Blank"**, Henry would go on to be a constant part of the BBC's Christmas line-ups every year. His first big hit on the channel was the fast-paced sketch series **"Three of A Kind"** with Tracey Ullman and David Copperfield which would never get its own Christmas special but did contribute to the all-new compendium show **"The Funny Side of Christmas"** (8:05pm, BBC One, December 27th 1982) as mentioned in the "Only Fools and Horses" chapter.[32] After fronting the comedy clip show **"Lenny Henry presents 'Laughing Matter'"** (9:45pm, BBC One, December 26th 1983) the following year he would introduce Bronski Beat, Slade, Bananarama, Black Lace, Ultravox and even Black Lace[33] in **"Top of the Pops' Review of 84"** (6:50pm, BBC One, December 27th 1984) as both himself

---

[32]   Henry had also become a Radio One DJ around this time with "The Lenny Henry Boxing Day Hoot!" appearing at noon on the same day "The Funny Side of Christmas" aired.

[33]   Nigel Planer would also appear in character as neil (always lowercase) from BBC Two's "The Young Ones" on which Henry had played an evil postman several months earlier.

and several of the characters from his first solo series "The Lenny Henry Show" including PC Ganja, newsreader Trevor McDoughnut and smooth as butter soul sensation Theophilus P. Wildebeeste.

He could be seen again on Christmas morning 1985 as part of the Comic Relief launch on **"The Noel Edmonds Live Live Christmas Breakfast Show"** and as part of an **"Omnibus"** repeat (11:10pm, BBC One, December 27th 1986) featuring the recorded live show put on by said charity before Red Nose Day became a thing. By the time Lenny's first solo Christmas special came round in 1987 he had already moved away from sketches to a sitcom about DJ and wide boy Delbert Wilkins which confusingly was also called "The Lenny Henry Show". **The Lenny Henry Christmas Special** (8pm, BBC One, December 24th 1987) featured Henry's strongest to date with Robbie Coltrane[34] joining Len for a savage takedown of American televangelists, cheapo telly channel JYTV's festive line-up, pensioner Deakus remembering warmer Christmases past (*"Sometimes me breath freezes...and in the morning I can see what I was saying in my sleep..."*) and a note-perfect ten minute parody of "The Rock N Roll Years" in which Henry performs his own take on The Temptations, Mungo Jerry, Hot Chocolate, Ike and Tina Turner (*"She took everything, she took my name...well, the first letter. I used to be called Mike Turner..."*) and Michael Jackson leading to the episode's most memorable moment - a spoof of Jackson's "Bad" complete with impressive latex mask to

---

[34] Lenny and Robbie would work together again on the serious one off "Screen One" drama "Live and Kicking" in October 1991 playing a desperate drug dealer and his tough social worker respectively.

make Henry resemble the era's "Wacko Jacko". It's a tour de force for Lenworth although particular respect is due to the man behind the music, the late Simon Brint, best known as the quiet half of Raw Sex.

"The Lenny Henry Special" (10:05pm, BBC One, December 26th 1988) followed with JYTV chasing Sky into the cheapo satellite television racket (*"deregulate! deregulate! beam! beam! Murdoch Murdoch!"*) before recreating "Who Framed Roger Rabbit?" with tragic results. 1988-centric material abounds about the Seoul Olympics, Bros and "Cheers" which is recreated perfectly for a very short but pointed sketch in which Lenny plays every single character bar Woody. An extended film pastiches gun toting action movies with Henry as "psycho cop from New Jersey" John Duck and once again the musical moments are note perfect with Lenny in drag as Whitney Houston with a drug test related rewrite of the US Olympic theme "One Moment in Time". The episode takes advantage of the later timeslot by closing with a new routine by slick soul smoothie Theophilus P. Wildebeeste bothering a woman from the crowd. It's a hip and reactive show made all the more stand out due to being followed by "Bruce and Ronnie", a famously buried bit of old school light entertainment featuring Forsyth and a newly single Corbett which many (including the acts themselves) expected to be a replacement for "The Two Ronnies". It's a pity as its quite good if a little dated in its dancing girls and shiny floor presentation but a world away from Lenny who'd had a huge year beginning with the first ever Red Nose Day which was celebrated in **"Comic Relief's Nose at Ten"** (10:10pm, BBC One, December 31st 1988)

It's easy to forget what an achievement Red Nose Day was when it launched in 1988. A day of being allowed to be silly for charity and then an entire evening given over to those naughty comedians you usually only got after 9pm on BBC Two. Occasionally the more traditional likes of Mike Yarwood, Little and Large and Ernie Wise might pop up but this was a night of wild live comedy with new mini-episodes of "Blackadder" and "The New Statesman", Harry Enfield's Stavros up the Telecom Tower, Michael Palin as a relation of his spiv Python character Dino Vercotti and Fry and Laurie in change of the gunge tank. Getting the comedians involved with the location filming was absolutely essential too in providing a recognisable guide to global problems and Lenny was at the heart of those, as well as anchoring the night with Griff Rhys-Jones and Jonathan Ross. There'd be a second Red Nose Day in 1989 before the wise decision was taken to make them bi-annual which it continues to this day with the 2021 event raising £52 million during one of the worst periods in history. Nothing to blow your (red) nose at.

Concentrating on stand-up and an ill-fated attempt at cracking the States, Lenny wouldn't be back on the seasonal small screen until the next decade but the production which heralded his return would be one of his best. A breezy comic adventure lasting just over an hour, **"Bernard and the Genie"** (8pm, BBC One, December 23rd 1991) features Henry as the manic, sword wielding Josephus freed from his lamp after 2000 years (*"2000 years? Most of my friends will be dead!"*) by naive but optimistic art dealer Bernard (Alan Cumming) who tries to do the right thing and is beaten by the world for it. What follows is a unambiguously joyful friendship as the Genie helps Bernard turn his life around while he enjoys the best of the modern world - which in 1991 meant going to see "Terminator 2" and eating everything in London (*"I'm glad dog meat is still popular!"*, says Josephus walking past a kebab stall) - before disaster strikes in the form of Rowan Atkinson playing a brilliantly slimy boss relishing the opportunity to use his full range of vocal tricks (*"That's a fully-fledged BASTARD of a point..."*) rolling a "B" in his mouth as if it's a bullet, together with a habit of needlessly saying "ye" in most sentences including the memorable "bugger ye off". Dennis Lill gets a similarly good turn as a loyal but constantly untruthful doorman (*"I had a friend who had both his legs blown off and he was up and walking around in a fortnight"*) who is perhaps Bernard's only true friend.

Director Paul Weiland keeps the story moving apace while Richard Curtis turns in one of his best scripts to date with Cumming and Henry both seemingly having a ball alongside some well-chosen cameos from Gary Lineker, Melvyn Bragg and Bob Geldof, all backed by the always excellent music by Howard Goodall. With all the hallmarks of a Christmas classic that could run and run it's deeply frustrating that boring rights issues meant it was only shown twice by BBC One. A big screen version has seemingly been on the cards since this first aired but presumably not including Lenny whose American movie debut "True Identity" had flopped hard. This may have explained a cameo in his next Christmas show **"Lenny Henry: In Dreams"** (9:30pm, BBC One, December 23rd 1992) an unusual but entertaining one-off vehicle in which Bill Paterson plays a therapist delving into Henry's subconscious allowing Len to investigate stranger avenues of comedy often connected to very real fears in the comic's life. One such sketch sees him crush three unpleasant newspaper hacks under his actually growing gargantuan bot; another finds Barry Norman popping up to critique his acting in a short film about going to the toilet titled "Bastard". Despite the condemnation, he next chose to return to sitcom for a fairly straight role Lil in **"Chef!"** starring Henry as the seemingly humourless, highly-strung cook of the title Gareth Blackstock. It was successful enough to gain three series and a 1993 Christmas Eve special where Blackstock and his wife disagree over suppliers at Christmas. As the fairly dry description proves, it was an adult sitcom in the grown-up sense with the first two runs on film and shot like a drama not dissimilar to the style that would become synonymous with Aaron Sorkin productions.

Having taken a few years away from traditional studio sketches **"The Lenny Henry Christmas Show"** (9:15pm, BBC One, December 28th 1994) was his grand return although it was a very different kind of show than he'd presented previously. Much as he had reinvented himself from his "New Faces" winning act to "Chef!", here was yet another shift to keep people on their toes. Shot 'as live' in front of an audience with more of a hip nightclub feel and a less family-targeted vibe, this was a bold move not least because Henry had dropped all of his popular characters for a new bunch of more topical ones including corrupt African ruler King Ade, hopeless Welsh rappers TWA (Taffies with Attitude) and the RuPaul-esque Amazonian model Deeva who teases the enormously stunned audience that were probably sat waiting for Delbert Wilkins to come on. The only sketch not performed live is a spot-on Blaxploitation spoof starring another new creation Nathan Gunn with a guest appearance by 'Jason King' himself, Peter Wyngarde.

Always a voice for pushing black culture to the forefront, Len used this new line-up to show more a more relevant take on the modern world that was unashamedly proud of its heritage. With music from Salt 'N' Pepa and Dina Carroll this was an intriguing if incredibly American-influenced new look from a face we'd known for nearly two decades. A series using the same style would launch on Saturday nights the following April but struggled to make the impact of his early work. Not that it seemed to bother Henry who was back the following Christmas with an entirely sketch based special, back pre-watershed and returning to some of the old favourite characters.

Soon he'd be trying on the hat of Saturday night family variety host for **"Lenny Henry Gets Wild"** (7pm, BBC One, December 28th 1996) and the subsequent series "Lenny Goes to Town" before returning yet again to sketches with a whole new range of characters in **"Lenny Henry in Pieces"** (9pm, BBC One, December 30th 2000) which was successful enough to run for another two years before being replaced by a new series once again called … "The Lenny Henry Show". After that came his biggest change yet as he became one of the country's leading dramatic actors. Lenny Henry is one of those people who are constantly worth watching or, in the case of his fantastic 2020 Radio 4 sketch series, listening to.

An underrated stand-up and a brilliant actor, it's fascinating how quickly some people will tell you they don't like Lenny Henry. And it is entirely their loss.

Game For A Quiz

With a year ravaged by pandemic and folks being unable to congregate as they regularly did, 2020 brought a lot to the fore about safety, sustainability and mental health conditions but as we hurtled towards December without any real changes and mostly confined to our homes, I started to wonder what the hell the TV was going to show on December 25th. The usual big entertainment spectaculars and dramas with huge casts I'd written about in previous, still very much available books were surely an impossibility?

Step forward our old pal the game show.

Already keeping the end up handsomely throughout the year due to the standard '400 in a week' recording blocks, quizzes and games were quick and easy to produce with contestants separated by Perspex or in the case of Michael McIntyre's surprisingly decent new series "The Wheel" strapped to a spinning fairground-style chair. Despite only being midway through its first series, BBC One would give it a prime 6pm slot on Christmas Day alongside a revival of "Blankety Blank" and a selection box from their light entertainment spectacular "Strictly Come Dancing". ITV similarly leant on "Tenable", "The Chase" and variety competition "Britain's Got Talent".

Between Christmas Eve and Boxing Day viewers to terrestrial channels could also see "Would I Lie to You?", "Alan Carr's Epic Gameshow", "Celebrity Crystal Maze", "Miranda's Games with Showbiz Names", "Tipping Point Lucky Stars", a thirty-year anniversary compilation of "Have I Got News for You", "The Wall Versus Celebrities", "The Big Soap Quiz", "Celebrity Catchphrase", "Family Fortunes", "Who Wants to Be a Millionaire?" and Channel Four's traditional "Big Fat Quiz of The Year". Just a few then.

Truly this was a golden time for quizzing and it reflected what many of us were doing on Zoom calls up and down the country. Quizzes are cheap, easy to make and a lot of fun as long as one of the participants isn't on mute. As a result, this section is a tribute to some of the quiz and game shows that filled our tiny boxes on Christmases past….

The eagle eyed amongst you will have spotted a few mentions of the life and works of Noel Edmonds in this book although very little so far about his long running **"Telly Addicts"** (1985-1998) which generally arrived as part of the new season of programmes in September and ran steadily up to December like a weekly bearded advent calendar with a grand final generally just before Christmas and a celebrity special just after. The first series in 1985 had been dominated by one family – the accurately titled Pains of Swindon – thanks to a "winner stays on" format and after they'd cleaned up in the final, they got the chance to take on a panel of "experts" including TV columnist Nina Myskow, the current host of "Points of View" Barry Took, Larry Grayson and the controller of BBC One Michael Grade. They clearly enjoyed it so much all four celebrities returned the year after to battle the 1986 champions. Grade was back in 1988, now as the recently appointed chief of Channel 4, taking on the BBC Managing Director Bill Cotton's team[35] with Ernie Wise, Susan Reynish from 1986's winning family plus a seemingly unannounced Leslie Grantham whose menacing appearance seems to throw the usually unflappable Noel for the first few

---

[35] Grade's team were nicknamed "The Grady Bunch". Cotton's team - comprising of with Terry Wogan, Tim Rice and TV critic Margaret Forwood – were "The Cotton Club" which seemingly ignored what the film they are named after was about. The Gradey Bunch won 27-24.

minutes. The regular quiz then continues as normal until towards the end of the show when some comedy police officers appear on set – again apparently without Noel's prior knowledge – to arrest 'Dirty Den'[36] Not surprisingly everyone points at Noel who is cuffed and carted off by the fuzz never to be seen again. It's basically Rodney King in bad knitwear.

Despite Noel continuing his jackbooted and garishly jumpered domination of our late Decembers he wouldn't be the first to try out this new TV related trivia game idea. An initial stab had been broadcast over Christmas 1984 as **"Telly Quiz"** (3:45pm, BBC Two, December 24th) hosted by comedian and former Lennie Bennett partner Jerry Stevens. With a strange reverse scoring system and an "ask the audience" style lifeline, it was a long way from the similarly titled "Pop Quiz" which hardy trivia fans could flip immediately over to that Christmas Eve. **"Pop Quiz Christmas Special"** (4:15pm, BBC One) hosted by Radio One and cringing's Mike Read would put two invariably baffling combinations of pop stars against each other in a trivia showdown. Here Noddy Holder, Toyah and a clearly desperate Meat Loaf took on Queen's Roger Taylor, Brian "Nasher" Nash from Frankie Goes to Hollywood and Green Gartside of Scritti Politti. Despite being a staple of Saturday nights, heavily merchandised and long associated with the eighties, few could guess Pop Quiz was only four days from its final BBC One episode – a legendary showdown between Duran Duran and Spandau Ballet – although short lived revivals would appear in 1994, 2008, 2011 and 2016.

---

36   Grantham's EastEnders character who at the time was in jail eventually being "killed off" in 1989.

People do love to see famous people either struggling or acing a quiz format because celebrities are obviously our natural superiors. Even the usually staid and only occasionally featuring a murderer Sunday afternoon darts quiz "Bullseye" would bring on the renowned faces for the festive period. And in 1990 the **"Bullseye Christmas Special"** (5:30pm, ITV, December 23rd) decided to slap an ill-fitting Dickensian theme onto proceedings too with host Jim Bowen in full Ebenezer Scrooge garb railing miserably at both the audience and the celebrity guests - Bobby Davro as Bob Cratchit, Bella Emberg his wife and Paul Shane essaying a not especially tiny Tiny Tim. Some Santa-hooded 'ghost' dartsmen Leighton Rees, Eric Bristow and Bob Anderson are also there to throw arrows and scorer Tony Green is dressed as Jacob Marley. All of which makes for a surreal half hour as everyone attempts to stay in character but also play the game for real. There's room for Davro to do his impressions including a lengthy section as Bowen himself and Emberg is the butt of some dire fat jokes as usual but most mesmerising of all is Paul Shane who looks half dead with biscuits round his mouth yet clearly also really wants to win and only breaks character at the very end.

It was a scene more suited to the strange miasma of rock-hard cryptic clues, pop singers, comedy turns, celebrity cameos, huge prizes and, of course, a giant comedy bin with a face on it that was "3-2-1". It should absolutely not have been a hit and yet with the warm, cheery presence of Ted Rogers at the helm it all seemed to just flow quite respectably leading to a ten year stay on TV. Each edition had a loose theme running throughout and so a **"3-2-1 Pantomime"** (5:05pm, ITV, December 25th 1980) wasn't a huge jump for audiences to expect. The panto in question was "Cinderella" from which suites would be acted out between rounds by Mike Reid doing his Mike Reid act as Buttons alongside Ted's fellow ITV game-show hosts Nicholas Parsons and Derek Batey playing the Ugly Sisters and a 'rapping' Bill Maynard as "The Slave of Dusty Bin". Adding to the "star quotient" was obese MP and (alleged) sex offender Cyril Smith.

With its infamous blindfolded sportsperson groping round, Smith would have clearly preferred[37] to be on naughty sports quiz **"They Think It's All Over"** (BBC One, 1995 - 2006) which managed three appearances on Christmas Day itself despite being rarely memorable or suited to the festive period in the slightest. With football becoming fashionable again with Nick Hornby's "Fever Pitch" being a success, the launch of the glossy "FourFourTwo" magazine and Baddiel and Skinner's "Fantasy Football League", it seemed a good time to launch a quiz named after one of the most famous commentator quotes of all time. As for the humour, time has probably not been kind to the schoolboy sniggering but seeing people known for being strait-laced like original panel captain Gary Lineker being encouraged into doing something rude could be greatly enjoyable. Although Lee Hurst definitely seemed a much better idea in the nineties.

Equally providing the 1990s 'sports' 'entertainment' was **"Gladiators: Celebrities Vs Jockeys"** (6:05pm, ITV, December 27th 1997) which posed some deep questions like "can a jockey be a celebrity?", "What makes a celebrity not a jockey?" and "blimey, is Gladiators still on?" The "that'll do" premise was appropriate for the state of the series at that point. For a time around 1992/93 it really was the biggest

---

[37] Because he loved sport! Not sure what you were thinking.

non-bearded thing in Saturday night entertainment with the competitors becoming household names - even if those names were things like Laser, Panther and Saracen. But now the sheen was long off the product with most of the original Gladiators gone and a bored post- "Shooting Stars" Ulrika Jonsson seems utterly disinterested in being there.

As for the famous people, there was Bradley Walsh - a long way from his current beloved status - who makes an awful joke about showering with the Gladiators but has an impressive run in the tennis ball-dodging "Danger Zone". Not far behind him is a 55-year-old jockey Willie Carson who makes a joke about his short stature meaning he'll be hard to catch. He is then caught within 3 seconds. After them Mark Speight, Bob Champion, Paul Ross, Peter Scudamore, Mr Motivator and the incomprehensible Tony Dobbin appear to push the word "celebrity" to its most finite level. Viewers who persisted at least got the pleasure of John Sachs commentary with lines like *"She tried to pull him off"*, *"his wife knows her Willie is just under five feet tall"* and *"Sam deciding to milk it over her some more"* without even a giggle in his voice.

Oh, and the Jockeys won. Well done jockeys.

For those who enjoyed their games with a lot less movement, BBC One had the **"Tomorrow's World Christmas Quiz"** (1986-92) in which the usual technology and science features were side-lined for some festive frippery hosted by the team's older brother- type Howard Stableford. Armed with some increasingly disagreeable seasonal jumpers and a series of groaner jokes (*"You know a lot about nuclear physics...I'll try not to 'fall out' with you then..."*) the quiz pitched a studio audience against on a panel headed up by a less obvious famous name such as Douglas Adams, David Bellamy and - not one but two Doctors Who (Whom?) - Colin Baker in 1986 and Sylvester McCoy in 1988, both in full costume, plus two genuine professionals from the scientific or medical worlds.

The central premise of the quiz remained more or less the same throughout the run – 'here's a thing and here's three different possibilities about what it might do' - an example in this episode being a leather strap which is intimated could be a hot air balloon 'holder downer', a didgeridoo holder or an easy hay bale grabber. Like most of its light entertainment schedule mates, there was plenty of room for more celebrities to pop on and shill their latest project with the 1991 show featuring the strange mix of Paul Merton, the cast of a live "Thunderbirds" stage show, an extremely uncomfortable David McCallum accompanied by a panto horse as promotion for the unpopular BBC horse racing drama "Trainer" and Anneka Rice who got to take on presenter James Burke in one of those old school virtual reality machines with the big chunky helmets that used to be so cool. Despite its cheesy presentation and stilted conversation in places, the "Tomorrow's World Christmas Quiz" was hard to dislike with a feel not dissimilar to teachers putting on a show and letting their hair down at the end of term. Sadly the 1992 show would be the final edition with the parent series coming to an end in 2003.

Much more BBC One's speed was **"That's Showbusiness!"** a light showbiz related panel game which seemed ever-present at one point, shifting from its initial good natured but dull tone in its early series with Gloria Hunniford and Kenny Everett as team captains to a more sarcastic "here's a photo of you looking slightly different!" yet still dull style by the end of its run in 1996. Mike Smith remained host throughout and the Christmas special from the 20th December 1993 is slap bang in the middle of this slightly arch shift as Michelle Collins and former "Casualty" actress Cathy Shipton take on Nigel Havers and Keith Barron who had both recently appeared together in the already cancelled ITV comedy drama "The Good Guys". All are ribbed in some ways - there's an appearance in a very early TV role for Collins where she looks…much the same, a perfectly acceptable 60s pop ballad to embarrass Havers who played on it, the mortified-looking Shipton gamely plays along when asked to dance the Can Can and a thoroughly miserable Barron is asked to recite Dickie Valentine's "Christmas Alphabet". The 1994 special starts with a joke I can best describe as "dated" about Gary Glitter and a giant prop described as the "John Wayne Bobbitt Memorial Shears" as Leslie Grantham and Brian Regan from "Brookside" look ready to murder. Which admittedly for both of them is quite fitting. From there it's surprisingly gets worse. It's a strange series that was very popular at the time but is forgotten now with a feel oddly foreshadowing Vic and Bob's **"Shooting Stars"** but with none of the genuine oddness.

That series had spawned out of **"At Home with Vic and Bob"** (7pm, BBC Two, December 27th 1993), a theme night Reeves and Mortimer prepared for BBC Two featuring a number of the duo's favourite programmes from the archive including a compilation of Eric Idle's terrific "Rutland Weekend Television", a rare 1972 Dad's Army sketch and Mike Leigh's incredibly funny play "Nuts in May"; plus original sketches from Pat Arrowsmith and Dave Wright: two regular fellers who just so happen to be wearing bras, troubled balladeers Mulligan and O'Hare and 1970s glam pop favourites "Slade" in their family home. Commissioned late in the year, the pair needed to come up with a lot of new material in less than a month so turned to Vic's Big Quiz, one of the few items from their pre-TV "Big Night Out" live shows that hadn't made it into any of their sketch series where Reeves would drag punters on stage and ask them nonsensical questions for mediocre prizes.

And thus a *"specially recorded quiz show in which Jonathan Ross, Wendy Richard[38] and Martin Clunes test celebrity-recognition skills against Danny Baker, Ulrika Jonsson and Noddy Holder"* was recorded as a fun but not especially outstanding one off. Had BBC Two not needed a filler half hour the following April it would've stayed a novelty too yet this pilot got surprisingly decent ratings outstripping the pair's sketch shows leading to a commission for eight episodes in 1995 with Ross replaced by stand-up comedian Mark Lamarr. Totalling eight series and 72 episodes over sixteen years and two revivals, "Shooting Stars" remains Vic and Bob's most enduring TV format. What works for BBC Two though doesn't necessarily translate to the big channel and though BBC One decided against poaching "Shooting Stars" for its own schedule, it did commission several brand-new formats from Reeves and Mortimer including the game show "Families at War". This was huge fun but probably a bit too strange for prime time and unable to find an audience in the

---

[38] To quote Bob's brilliant 2021 autobiography "And Away": "Wendy Richard got very impatient with the process and threw a bit of a strop. Jim told her to cheer up and stop acting like she'd just received her gas bill." "Mondo Rosso", a Ross-hosted tribute to cult movies also debuted the same night as "Shooting Stars" on September 22nd 1995.

middle of summer. It felt like a try out as a replacement for an increasingly worn out "Generation Game" which had been revived with original host Bruce Forsyth at the helm in September 1991. Bruce returned to the Beeb after a decade away for the bizarre prize-stealing game show "Takeover Bid" but when that didn't gel with viewers the BBC's Head of Light Entertainment Jim Moir suggested they have another crack at the super-popular 1970s family spectacular format. Initially going out on Friday nights, the rejuvenated series was almost identical to the original and soon built up its audience week by week resulting in 16.73 million looking in on **"Bruce's Christmas Generation Game"** (6:25pm, BBC One, December 25th 1991).

A much-needed blast of old school light entertainment with features that could – and did – turn up in the original twenty years previous with handbell ringing, the audience being encouraged to sing "A Bicycle Made for Two", a ballet sketch not dissimilar to the act Forsyth was doing at the London Palladium 35 years prior and everyone gathering round a piano at the end to sing "White Christmas". Not everything works - some of the patter would be a hashtag waiting to happen in the modern age - but it's the games and challenges at the heart of the show that still drive it forward as regular members of the public get the chance to try new things and act hilariously badly alongside cameos from comedian Kenny Lynch, Neighbours' Madge and Harold (Anne Charleston and Ian Smith) and the actual real Captain Birdseye off the adverts. Forsyth constantly reminds us throughout why he's at the top of his game and it's hard not to grin at daft throwaway lines like *"You design golf courses, jails and hotels…So its links, clinks and 40 winks…"* The success of this special meant the "Generation Game" remained at the heart of Christmas schedules for the next few years until Jim Davidson took over and ruined it. But there'd be more Brucie bonuses on Christmas Day a decade later as "Strictly Come Dancing" became another huge hit in a sixty-year career full of them. Didn't they do right good and that?

Naturally, all of these are mere postscripts to the real giant in the field, a title that defined the genre and brought television trivia screaming into the modern age. I am undeniably referring to **"Farming Diary - So You Think You Know About Farming?"** (1:40pm, ITV, December 23rd 1973) which the TV Times described as "the most difficult in the young farmer's calendar." Sadly, the contents of this were not recorded and painstakingly converted to YouTube for me to check so I'll have to defer to the TV Times again for more information: *"Ten contestants, one from each area Federation, battle with each other for Farming Diary's coveted award the Silver Bull which will be presented by this year's Miss Anglia."* And if that isn't the true spirit of Christmas, my friends, I don't know what is…

Hey! A Movie! The Eighties

1980

It's the eighties! Big hair! Funny Eddie Murphy! A Day-Glo sock! So, what have the channels got for us on Christmas Day? Why it's the network premiere of 1954's Disney adventure **"20,000 Leagues Under the Sea"** (3:10pm) featuring ol' bot chin Kirk Douglas as "master-harpooner" Ned Land and James Mason as Captain Nemo. A passion project of Walt Disney himself, this Jules Verne adaptation came in at a shade over two hours providing excellent napping opportunities for turkey-stuffed grandads everywhere before "The Paul Daniels Magic Show". Once suitably enlivened by the works of Grayson, Yarwood and the Dallas cast, viewers were allowed to strap and feel the Gs in "Airport 1975" (8:45pm) which confusingly was made in 1974. This would spearhead a number of big budget disaster porn spectaculars including **"The Towering Inferno"** on the BBC and **"Earthquake"** overlapping on ITV as each side's big Boxing Day film the day after.

After the standard biggest dog in the world antics of 1973's **"Digby - the Biggest Dog in the World"** at 11:40am, viewers were greeted by more home-grown comedy in the afternoon with the big screen spin-off movie of ITV sitcom **"George and Mildred"** (3:10pm). Despite being based on one of their own properties, this was an unusual premiere due to the relative newness of the film which only left theatres several months earlier. Having done very little business on the big screen, in part due to the death of co-star Yootha Joyce just before its release, it was quickly sped onto its more familiar medium. Sadly, like most sitcom offshoot films it is bleedin' awful. Much more stirring was the latest James Bond premiere **"The Man with the Golden Gun"** (6pm) from 1974 and the Glenda Jackson-starring romantic comedy **"A Touch of Class"** at 10:40pm except for those twelve regions who went with **"Liza Minnelli in Concert in New Orleans"** instead. ITV also got in first showings of Alfred Hitchcock's final film **"Family Plot"** (1976) and 1965's **"Dr Zhivago"** which comfortably filled over three and a half hours on New Year's Day.

And for fans of Fred Astaire, you can watch some films with him moving his legs in that way you like on BBC Two with Bing Crosby in 1946's **"Blue Skies"** (4:10pm) and the spectacular 'musical about a musical' **"The Band Wagon"** from seven years later at 6:05pm. Sending viewers to bed with a wry smile, Billy Wilder directs a seemingly never far apart Jack Lemmon and Walter Matthau in **"The Front Page"** at 10:30pm. And that is the newwwwwssss.

1981

More death and destruction on the Beeb with a Christmas Eve unleashing of **"The Poseidon Adventure"** and a second Jules Verne adaptation – the 1961 Disney adventure **"In Search of the Castaways"** (4:10pm) taking the traditional family film slot. This clashed in part with a repeat showing of the first Bond outing **"Dr No"** (3:15pm) on ITV as the network realised how many more viewers they could bring in with Bond premieres happening away from the busy spotlight of Christmas Day. As such it was all a warm up act for **"The Muppet Movie"** (5:50pm) which lit the lights later that day just two years after it had been a hit in cinemas thanks in part to being co-produced by Lew Grade who co-owned ITV's Midlands franchise ATV and had backed "The Muppet Show" years earlier when America wasn't interested.

This early appearance on the box had caused controversy due to the gentleman's agreement television had with cinema distributors to allow a grace period of at least five years between big and small screen showings of a film. But as ATV had lost their licence[39] and were going off air six days later, I don't think he much gave a stuff.

Also popping up for ITV would be **"Close Encounters of The Third Kind"** (1978) which they chose to hold back until the 28th December while BBC One would similarly defer the premiere of 1939's epic **"Gone with the Wind"** over two nights much like "Lawrence of Arabia" in 1975. The film's 221-minute girth spread comfortably over Boxing Day and December 27th, easily becoming BBC One's biggest film of the festive period. Not too hard when Christmas night's movie was a brand new but totally forgotten heist drama starring Albert Finney named **"Loophole"** (9:25pm) airing almost simultaneously with the similarly heist themed comedy **"Harry and Walter Go To New York"** (9:35pm)

BBC Two meanwhile gave the people what they wanted – an encore showing of **"Dersu Uzala"** (7pm) from 1975. Before that Harold Lloyd made his semi-regular festive appearance with 1925's **"The Freshman"** (2:05pm) ahead of the 1961 Chinese animation **"Uproar in Heaven"**[40] (3:35pm) which

---

[39] In part due to his involvement but that's a much more complicated story for a little book like this...

[40] Also known as "Havoc in Heaven", it had been produced originally in two parts during 1961 and 1964.

may have seemed familiar to Western audiences as the basis for the dubbed "Monkey" series which was being broadcast by BBC Two on Friday teatimes and based on the same source material of Wu Cheng'en's 16th century novel "Journey to the West". Two also had a Jack Lemmon season with his quirky 1972 comedy **"The War Between Men and Women"** making its first TV appearance on Christmas night at 11:15pm. I think it ended up a draw.

1982

Oh, hello Channel Four, I see you've joined the party. And you've brought some old films to show us all, including another Buster Keaton season and nearly three hours of **"Richard III"** (9pm) starring Laurence Olivier and John Gielgud on Christmas night. There's even a first production by the new Children's Film Unit – **"Captain Stirrick"** (10:30am) – all about Victorian pickpockets. Running from 1981 to early 2000s, the Unit actively encouraged children between 10 and 16 to get involved and learn about filmmaking. The young uns might possibly enjoy Anthony Newley as **"Mister Quilp"** (12:05pm), a strange, forgotten 1975 musical based around Charles Dickens' "The Old Curiosity Shop" which provided one half of a Pops 'n' Queen sandwich for BBC One with horse-based melodrama **"International Velvet"** (3:05pm) at the other side. In the evening Peter Ustinov stuck on the moustache again as Hercule Poirot in the entertaining but lengthy **"Death on the Nile"** (8:15pm) from 1978. Whether the 2022 Kenneth Branagh version will improve upon matters remains to be seen…

It was quite the contrast to Disney's **"The Black Hole"** (8pm) on ITV. Or at least it was if you lived outside the South West of England where TSW decided to ditch the so-so sci-fi effort in favour of Alan Arkin comedy **"The In-Laws"**. Another Disney live-action film **"The Parent Trap"** (3:05pm) had been left more or less alone however in post-Queen position.

Billy Wilder's penultimate film **"Fedora"** (10:40pm) took the late slot on BBC Two and earlier **"The Millionairess"** (5:20pm) aired as part of the channel's big theme season "Sellers Over Christmas. There's also room throughout the week for a series of early morning "Tarzan" films and some of Elvis' less awful musicals on BBC One.

1983

Quite possibly the most bizarre line-up of films made up a strange schedule which stood side by side with bonus religion due to the 25th landing on a Sunday in 1983. No less than four films made it onto BBC One with the best being the latest live action film let out of the Disney vault **"Treasure Island"** (3:05pm) Before that however was the miserable double bill of Australian flop **"The Little Convict"** (11:20am) and British sci-fi oddity **"The Glitterball"** (1:05pm) The former begins with Rolf's signature hit-that-isn't-about-boys "Jake the Peg" before he goes on to tell the incredibly dull part-animated tale about a young British boy sent on a convict ship headed for New South Wales. Kids must have thrilled to the scene where an old man is crushed to death by a tree. Amazingly it failed to recoup its budget at the Australian box office. With "Star Wars" the big hit of

1977, "The Glitterball" was on hand as a shitter, cheaper version of space thrills featuring a bleeping ball-bearing and very little actual space or thrills. Despite that this was one of the less tedious specials the BBC would dredge up in the mid-80s when they'd completely maxed out their kids TV budget but it's now probably more interesting as a historical document guide to what high street shops and kid's fashions looked like in the late-seventies.

Once again the evening film was from the same year as broadcast with 1983's **"Better Late Than Never"** (10:15pm) starring the recently deceased David Niven. Also practically gleaming was Channel 4's evening premiere **"The King of Comedy"** (8:25pm) which had quickly arrived and left cinemas in summer 1983. For those who haven't seen Scorsese's dark comedy, it's a moody, tense and troubled film about delusional people pushed to extreme acts so, y'know, clearly a Christmas movie. Robert De Niro nails the sketchy Pupkin, making him neither a total loser nor a psychopath, while a stunning 27-year-old Sandra Bernhard is perfect as a celebrity obsessed stalker and Pupkin's closest contact to anything approaching reality. Even the late, grating Jerry Lewis as the target of both their attentions, chat host Langford, is actually bearable. I suspect more people saw it on Channel 4 than anywhere prior and it was certainly a lively alternative to **"Revenge of the Pink Panther"** (9:10pm) on ITV at the same time and their only new film after a re-run of **"Superman"** (3:15pm) in the afternoon. Channel 4 also gave the first UK showing to Jacques Tati's silent comedy classic **"Les Vacances de Monsieur Hulot"** (4:25pm) or "Monsieur Hulot's Holiday" to you chum.

BBC Two outdid themselves with **"Meet Me in St. Louis"** (4:25pm) part of a range of films celebrating Judy Garland and a separate season of late-night Marx Brothers films with **"Duck Soup"** (11pm) on the menu that night. Later in the week the original three Harry Palmer films – **"The Ipcress File"** (1965), **"Funeral in Berlin"** (1966) and **"Billion Dollar Brain"** (1967) – got an always welcome run out.

1984

One of those films you just can't imagine not being on at Christmas, 1984 was the first year **"Mary Poppins"** (3:10pm) made it to telly alongside another showing of **"Some Like It Hot"** (10:55pm) in BBC One's "All Time Great Movies" season. Practically perfectly, Mary would demolish **"The Man with The Golden Gun"** (3:10pm) which was having a second trip out on the 25th as ITV were saving their whip-cracking heft for **"Raiders of the Lost Ark"** (8:30pm) which would bring in a whopping 19.35m viewers on Christmas night. By the far the most successful film of the week, it did oddly tie for the top overall with a BBC sitcom repeat of the first "Porridge" Christmas episode "No Way Out" shown two days later. The next two Indy films would end up at the Beeb with "Temple of Doom" on Christmas Day 1987 and "The Last Crusade" the same date five years later. They also apparently showed some fourth film on New Year's Day 2011 but I refuse to believe this exists.

BBC Two was dominated in the evening by over three hours of **"Kaos"** (1984), a subtitled anthology of Luigi Pirandello short stories directed by Paolo and Vittorio Taviani which was definitely a counterpoint to The Two Ronnies and Indy on the other side. Earlier in the day there had been a little more levity with not one but two films in its latest Charlie Chaplin season – **"A Dog's Life"** (1:55pm) and **"Limelight"** (3:25pm) a few hours later. Channel 4 had no theme season with highlights including another Jacques Tati comedy **"Jour de fête"** (1:50pm) and their own newly produced **"The Young Visiters"** (3:20pm) based on the Daisy Ashford poem and featuring the recent breakout star Tracey Ullman.

1985

After a decade of escalating bigger movie wars, it's surprising to note how few new films showed up in 1985 on Christmas Day as homemade feature-length episodes of existing shows ruled the roost with "All Creatures Great and Small", "Only Fools and Horses" and "Minder on the Orient Express" each taking up the space traditionally reserved for a much more expensive movie licence. The films that did appear weren't particularly classic either as BBC One stuck out **"The Gnome Mobile"** (10:05am) for a second time on Christmas morning with nothing until the possibly misjudged Sydney Pollack thriller **"Absence of Malice"** at 10:40pm at the other end of the day. Disney's **"The Black Hole"** (11:15am) made yet another appearance before lunch on ITV with another repeat in the afternoon courtesy of **"Moonraker"** (3:05pm). Even their late film, the wonderful **"Gregory's Girl"** (10:50pm), had been on Channel 4 first earlier in the year.

Luckily film fans were still very well served by BBC Two and Channel 4, the former of which paid tribute to the newly deceased Orson Welles with **"Citizen Kane"** (4:30pm) as part of a "Welles Directs" season. There was also Fred Astaire's final TV role in the 1978 telemovie **"The Man in the Santa Claus Suit"** (12:20pm) and the premiere of quirky French musical thriller **"Diva"** (10pm). Movie mavens could also enjoy "Film Buff of the Year" beforehand with an 'All-Winners Show' answering questions on topics as varied as Hollywood musicals of the 1940s to French New Wave director Claude Chabrol.

Over on Four, it was a feast of black and white with **"The Marx Brothers at The Circus"** (2:35pm), Buster Keaton in 1940's **"Nothing but Pleasure"** (4:15pm) and three hours of Douglas Fairbanks in 1924's silent swashbuckler **"The Thief of Bagdad"** (4:45pm) The station also offered a season of films from British duo Frank Launder and Sidney Gilliat, the most famous probably being their screenplay for 1938's "The Lady Vanishes" directed by Alfred Hitchcock.

1986

A milestone for ITV and British telly in general as **"Dumbo"** (3:10pm) becomes the very first animated Disney film to air in full on British TV easily whupping rival **"Annie – The Musical"** (also 3:10pm) on the BBC with 14 million viewers. Weirdly the evening's 1983 Bond premiere **"Never Say Never Again"** (6:30pm) would not only fail to deliver enough viewers to make ITV's weekly top 30 programmes but also get beaten comfortably by a repeat showing of **"The Spy Who Loved Me"** the following day. As such not a single Bond film since has made its terrestrial debut on the 25th again to this day.

With an evening packed with Trotters, Miss Marple and two flipping episodes of "EastEnders" the BBC's next film wouldn't be until 10:40pm when the day ended with Julie Walters charmed the nation with **"Educating Rita"**. Nearly 13.9 million choosing to stay up for it over another showing of director Billy Wilder's **"Fedora"** (11:10pm) on BBC Two and another Agatha Christie adaptation – the Poirot US TV movie **"Dead Man's Folly"** (10:10pm) - on ITV. Two would also slot in Wilder's **"The Fortune Cookie"** from 1966 (5:15pm) as part of a retrospective. And does BBC Two have a lengthy subtitled drama in the evening? You know it! This time its **"Edith and Marcel"** (8:20pm), a 1983 French biopic about the romance between singer Edith Piaf and boxer Marcel Cerdan. Over on Channel Four just one big proper film made the schedules – 1941's freewheeling musical comedy **"Hellazpoppin'"** (1:25pm)

Fans of movie classics like that would definitely have enjoyed BBC One's Barry Norman-hosted series of movie classics that week shown under the banner title of…um, "Movie Classics". BBC Two got a bit carried away with tribute seasons to the recently deceased Anna Neagle and Vincente Minnelli before Christmas while the still-quite-living-for-the-moment-thank-you David Lean and the aforementioned Wilder waited in the wings.

1987

Indiana Jones is back but this time he's on BBC One with **"Indiana Jones and the Temple of Doom"** - a film hideously unsuited for the 3:40pm time slot but comfortably the biggest film of the week with 18.95m tuned in. That would be it however for films until James L Brooks' comic weepie **"Terms of Endearment"** at 10:40pm although more "Movie Classics" would follow later in the week including "The Maltese Falcon" and "Twelve Angry Men".

ITV decided to counter with some mouse eared big guns starting with the wonderful short **"Mickey's Christmas Carol"** (11am) before another chance to see "Dumbo" (11:30am). After The Queen a double bill of **"Alice in Wonderland"** (3:10pm) and **"Bedknobs and Broomsticks"** (4:35pm) took the channel comfortably into the evening with only another showing of **"The Spy Who Loved Me"** (12:40pm) and **"Airplane II: The Sequel"** (12:15am) not being provided by the House of Mouse.

BBC Two had a music heavy schedule in 1987 with only 1945's Christmas comedy oddity **"The Cheaters"** (9:10am) and the traditional **"White Christmas"** (10:35am) recognisably films. They'd join a 1982 Franco Zeffirelli adaptation of Verdi's "La Traviata" starring Placido Domingo at 3:10pm. Even Channel 4 only had two proper films all day – Sean Connery in 1982's depressing and quite incest-themed **"Five Days One Summer"** (6:45pm) and the hip hop showcase **"Wild Style"** at 1:25am. Curse you "the arts"!

1988

Falling again on a Sunday, two of 1985's best action comedies were called in by BBC One to prop up an otherwise oddly muted Christmas with comic Western **"Silverado"** in the evening (9:20pm) and the still fantastically exciting **"Back to

The Future" (3:10pm) being seen by 14.9m great Scotts. There's also room before bed for an entry in their "Broadway Musicals" season with 1956's **"Carousel"** (11:40pm) although this would clash with another Christmas Day appearance of **"Some Like It Hot"** (12:20am) now over on BBC Two. This would be scheduled after – you guessed it – a respected foreign film with subtitles, this time the 1987 Italian drama **"The Family"** (10:15pm) which spanned several time periods but sadly without use of a DeLorean car. In the week following, Two would also dedicate a daily slot to both great British comedies such as "The Ladykillers" and "Passport to Pimlico" and also the work of Humphrey Bogart, although his movies are so synonymous with the festive period, you'd be hard pressed to notice any difference.

Just one major film for ITV thanks to an extra-long "London's Burning" and a Dame Edna special but when you've got the first showing of **"The Empire Strikes Back"** (3:55pm) that's sometimes all you need...even if it was beaten in the ratings by "The Bill". They were at least running 24 hours a day by this point with a "Christmas Night at the Movies" thread which would run for the next few years even if it was back to a choice of films depending whereabouts you were in the country.

Even Channel 4 also only had one film on its mostly music and documentary packed schedule and if you guessed it was a 1929 black and white silent comedy -the mild Hollywood satire **"Show People"** (2pm), go get yourself an extra helping of sprouts! Parp!

1989

And as we leave the eighties, **"Crocodile Dundee"** (6:15pm) puts a film at the top of the ratings for the first time in five years as 21.77 million tuned into BBC One for Paul Hogan and his much-discussed knife collection. John Cleese's brilliant farce **"Clockwise"** (10:20pm) would be the only other film on the books that day but as 1980's comedy films go, they're definitely two of the best.

Clearly jealous of Channel 4 and their sweet range of crackly black and white movies, BBC Two put out Alexander Korda's "Marseille Trilogy" over three days starting with 1931's **"Marius"** (3pm) before moving on, as we all know, to 1932's "Fanny". Stop it. The traditional subtitled film would this year be **"Babette's Feast"** (7:50pm) a beautifully shot Danish character piece from 1987 that had won the 'Best Foreign Language Film' Oscar the previous year. A "Viva Leone!" season paid tribute to the deceased Sergio with a premiere of 1973's comic spaghetti Western **"My Name Is Nobody"** at 10:40pm.

Over on the third button, two Roald Dahl stories were central to both Christmas and Boxing Day with "Danny the Champion of the World" on the latter and a glorious new animated adaptation of **"The B.F.G."** (3:15pm) by Cosgrove Hall on Christmas afternoon. I don't think I truly appreciated its slow, gentle nature at the time but it's an inventive and playful film full of Whizzpoppers and Snozzcumbers - where the Dream Country is as sparkly and psychedelic as the real world is ugly and unkind, all of it incredibly faithful to the original book's macabre and magical words. A richly-animated, fantastical sloshfunking tale for phizzwizards of all ages which couldn't be more different from ITV's other premiere of the day – the very adult 1986 social class comedy **"Down and Out in Beverly Hills"** (9pm) which ITV would be oddly fond of over the coming years. Oh, and the Bond film was **"On Her Majesty's Secret Service"** at 12:25pm, an odd farewell to the decade that made Bond films on Christmas Day such a recognisable trope for years to come.

Channel 4's two films for the day were both tributes to the recently deceased Laurence Olivier with the 1940 adaptation of **"Pride and Prejudice"** (1:10pm) and once again his lengthy **"Richard III"** (9pm) was unfurled for all to admire. I'm saluting like a trooper.

Sketchy People

Whilst the relatively cheap and easy quiz formats have thrived over the previous decade a genre that has become much rarer in the wake of smaller audiences, tighter budgets and less need to provide a big alternative to the BBC "Nine O' Clock News" since it moved an hour later is the sketch show. These were everywhere when I was growing up from prime-time family comics like Russ Abbot or Cannon and Ball to the naughtier alternative comedy shows I was sneakily watching on my black and white portable.

One such series, perhaps the gold standard of sketch shows for many, was **"Monty Python's Flying Circus"** which never had a festive special despite episodes from series one, two and three airing around Christmas week despite having nothing to do with the season. The series three episode which appeared on December 21st 1972 would in fact be the most censored to date with several items removed by order of BBC management and yet still managed a lengthy sketch set in a Tudor porn shop and another about unhinged vicars. That was still relatively tame compared to the final episode of the second series from December 22nd 1970 which climaxed in the infamous "Undertaker" sketch. Here a mortician played with ghoulish relish by Graham Chapman suggests that John Cleese's customer might like to eat his recently deceased mother with the option of throwing her up into a grave later if he feels remorse. At this point members of the studio audience are seen to angrily storm the stage in an alarmingly realistic fashion. They are only stopped from assaulting the actors and causing a full riot when the National Anthem is played, the pay off to a running joke throughout the episode about the Queen potentially tuning in for the show at some point during the evening. The Rev. Francis Coveney wrote to the Radio Times to "seriously suggest that people who can think up this sort of rubbish should consult a psychoanalyst before they proceed any further."[41] His reaction to the line *"You wouldn't know the difference between the Battle of Borodino and a tiger's bum"* - also in this episode – remains sadly unrecorded.

It's a shame there was never a proper Python Christmas special as several of the cast had already been involved in a particularly excellent one several years earlier. **"Do Not Adjust Your Stocking"** (4:10pm, ITV, December 25th 1968) was a special, extended edition of the "Fairly Pointless Show" for younger audiences "Do Not Adjust Your Set". This quickly became the stuff of legend as one of those quintessential "rush home from work to see it" shows inviting a mental image of poor pin-striped, bowler hatted chaps stuck on buses wishing they were watching the latest episode of "Captain Fantastic", a character played by the diminutive David Jason. Also on the team was the always hilarious Denise Coffey and three well educated young men named Michael Palin, Terry Jones and Eric Idle.

It's a cheap and cheerful sketch show for kids that much like the Pythons' later work, revels in wordplay and confounding expectations with support from the extravagant, colourful (even in black and white!) Bonzo Dog Band. This festive chapter also showcased new member of the team Terry Gilliam and his animated short "The Christmas Card". You

---

[41] With the reaction the original footage had received by the real public this final sketch was ear-marked for removal from future repeats. As such, when it came to releasing the episodes on VHS, the original recording had seemingly disappeared and a lower quality 525-line NTSC broadcast copy from US television had to be spliced in giving an eerie out-of-reality glow to the already unsettling scene.

have to wonder what kids thought in 1969 when they saw the names of their teatime heroes next to some weirdly titled circus show at 11 o'clock on a Sunday night.

Seven years later Idle would progress to his very own series purporting to feature the line-up of Britain's smallest independent TV station. Made on an actual shoestring budget, the cheap and cheerful nature of the premise was also somewhat of a necessity although Idle had a deep enough address book to ensure some excellent support from his old "Do Not Adjust Your Set" cast mate and ex-Bonzo Dog Neil Innes. They're joined in **"Christmas with Rutland Weekend Television"** (10:55pm, BBC Two, December 26th 1975) by a chap named George Harrison. Naturally there's a caveat to getting a Beatle on your series and here it's that he wants to perform in a pirate sketch against the wishes of Idle. Elsewhere, there's a lesson on How to Ski in Your Own Home, Innes performing "I Don't Believe in Santa Any More" and "Rutland Film Night" with a savage but slyly appreciative look at a familiar looking new rock musical named "Pommy" ("He'll tear your ears apart") featuring another Innes original, "Concrete Jungle Boy", a Who pastiche as good as anything in "Tommy". The show ends with the return of Harrison, free of his earlier pirate costume, ready to sing his No.1 hit "My Sweet Lord". Or is he...?

The idea of a Beatle in a comedy show wasn't the most far-fetched suggestion. Paul McCartney would later turn up on "The Mike Yarwood Christmas Show" and "Bread" while Ringo was seemingly available for three bob on and a sandwich to anyone who asked nicely. Peter Cook and Dudley Moore were equally charming on **"Not Only.... But Also"** (9pm, BBC Two, December 26th 1966) The spiky but loving relationship between the two was instantly popular with viewers and two series aired in 1965 and 1966 before this Boxing Day special which thankfully remains one of the only existing editions after years of thankless tape wiping. This comes as great relief to Beatle fans being as it features John Lennon[42] as the doorman to the hottest private members club in town the 'Ad Lav'[43] which also happened to be a public convenience. The real highlight of the episode also had a touch of The Beatles about it with the affectionate but brutal pastiche of psychedelic pop "The L.S Bumblebee". Despite the rather un-Fabs sounding cries of "Oh druggy druggy!" and "freak out baby, the bee is coming!" – not to mention the rather more obvious joke in that it says "bum" a lot – the legend goes that less clued up or perhaps simply mischievous US DJs picked up on the song and played it as a track from the new Beatles LP which was bootlegged accordingly for years. Unlike many sixties' music parodies, it's easy to see why people might have been fooled due to its gorgeous production and genuinely catchy tune[44].

Cook would appear on Boxing Day again twenty-four years later in **"A Life in Pieces"** (9:50pm, BBC Two, December 26th 1990) as the multi-purpose aristocrat, failed restaurateur and bore Arthur Streeb-Greebling, a character initially found on "Not Only…But Also". This time, interviewed by Ludovic Kennedy, he'd record a dozen five-minute pieces

---

[42]   He previously appeared on the "Not Only…But Also" pilot recorded in November 1964.

[43]   A spoof of the real-life swinging hotspot the 'Ad Lib' club.

[44]   It was released as a single by Decca the following January backed with Pete and Dud's anti-drug talk "The Bee Side."

vaguely connected to the 12 days of Christmas. Not his career best but it was good to see Cook on TV being funny in a late resurgence that would soon be capitalised upon with memorable appearances on "Have I Got News for You", "Clive Anderson Talks Back" and back in the guise of Sir Arthur for an obscure but wonderful Radio 3 series called "Why Bother?" with young, aggressive inquisitor and collaborator Chris Morris.

Also, trandom cycling from the Cambridge Footlights that had produced both Cook and Anderson were Bill Oddie, Graeme Garden and Tim Brooke-Taylor, collectively known as The Goodies who racked up a number of memorable Christmas specials over the seventies. Though it could be argued the fast-paced comedy was more of a sitcom due to its consistent characters, the free-wheeling nature of the series was merely a framework to throw daft gags, advert parodies, musical spoofs and in **"The Goodies and the Beanstalk"** (5:15pm, BBC Two, December 24th 1973) a full on film pastiche of pantomime tropes. It's one of the series most memorable episodes, in part due to a cameo by John Cleese in his "and now for something completely different" announcer mode, heckling them with "KID'S SHOW!", acknowledging the subversive appeal of The Goodies' to a young audience. Its huge fun and only slightly pipped in quality by **"The Goodies Rule - OK?"** (7:25pm, BBC Two, December 21st 1975) which is perhaps the most ambitious episode of the series which begins as a spoof on pop stardom and ends with the trio being attacked by TV puppets including - yes - the giant Dougal and Zebedee from "The Magic Roundabout".

There'd be a festive twinge to the final episode of series six **"Earthanasia"** (9pm, BBC Two, December 22nd 1977) during which the trio discover at half eleven on Christmas Eve that the world is going to end at midnight. Pretty much done in real time on one set with only the three leads, it's a superb, creative and hilarious if not especially Christmassy show which would've been the perfect end to the series had they decided to stop there. The shows were still rating highly though and thus, after a two-year break, what would turn out to be their last series arrived on the BBC in 1980. Frustrated by delays allegedly due to the Beeb's in house visual effects team being distracted by the TV adaptation of "The Hitchhikers Guide to The Galaxy" the threesome found themselves won over by LWT and a healthy cheque book.

Until the release of a DVD containing all their episodes for ITV, it had been long received wisdom this one series for the commercial channel was vastly inferior. In fact, it might be their strongest run of episodes in years, kicking off with the Superchaps Three joining the seven dwarves as "Soppy, Grotty and... Tim" in the surprisingly dark **"Snow White 2"** (7:15pm, ITV, December 27th 1981) ripping apart everything from video nasties to pantomime cows and sexual equality in the female-led world of panto roles. As a genuinely unnerving horror pastiche on pre-watershed telly, it wouldn't be beaten until **"Christmas Night with the Two Ronnies"** (7:25pm, BBC One, December 25th 1987)

This would be the final regular edition of the beloved series before Ronnie Barker retired from TV and rather than play it safe went out on a high with a 17 minute "Pinocchio II: Killer Doll" sketch where Gepetto makes a second wooden boy from an evil tree sprite. The look of the film is perfect from costumes to set dressing, the music cues could come from any British video horror nasty of the era, the guest cast are superb and, amazingly, even features Charlton Heston in a brief cameo. The problem is it all actually works TOO well and, despite the gags, it is truly unsettling at times with the scratchy dark old film taking viewers a million miles away from the bright studio lights in the rest of the episode. The sketch ends with a demonic Corbett laughing hysterically as Gepetto burns to death. Merry Christmas everybody! The twosome would return one last time to the 25th December, sadly after Barker's death, in 2005's best of "The Two Ronnies' Christmas Sketchbook" which wisely left out "Pinocchio II" in favour of some less stool loosening festive fare from their extensive back catalogue.

Not all exits from television around this time were as good natured however. First getting his own ATV sketch series in 1968, comic impressionist Mike Yarwood could be seen on one channel or another for another two decades and his Christmas Day special in 1977 is considered to have just pipped Morecambe and Wise slightly as around 28 million people watched both shows on the BBC. When the double act quit for ITV the following year, Yarwood got the prime slot and comfortably beat them at their new commercial home. And yet… considering his peak popularity, it's strange how little he actually means to anyone under the age of forty. Partly this is because the topicality of his act makes his back catalogue of impressions near impenetrable in the modern age with a high level of political figures now long dead. A female prime minister also scuppered him a little but looking back, his programmes are just a bit too slow for a modern audience and **"The Mike Yarwood Christmas Show"** (8pm, ITV, December 21st 1982) saw him fail to heed the folly of Eric and Ernie as he followed the money over to Thames at the end. Despite being his first festive performance since defecting from the Beeb, the episode fails to investigate any new ideas and falls back on the same old impersonations with his Prince Charles featured in a spoof interview with Selina Scott and a 13-minute Ronald Reagan sketch which creaks more than the jokes about his age which are plentiful here, with none of the warmongering and crass ignorance that other satirical programmes would mine so successfully throughout the decade.

The most successful item is probably the takedown of one of ITV's biggest hits of the time "Game for a Laugh". Sadly, though the gags are decent enough (*"the belly dancing vicar from Stoke Poges with his yodelling tortoise..."*) his Matthew Kelly impersonation is mostly comedy homosexual. It's a sketch that feels like it could smoothly slot into David Renwick and Andrew Marshall's magnificent TV-spoofing sketch show "End of Part One" so it's little surprise to see the former's name come up as head writer when the credits roll. The gentler, whimsical way Mike Yarwood treated his subjects proved not to be what the 80s audiences were looking for as the Falklands war, mass unemployment, the miner's strikes and growing public unrest made many eager for a bit of edge to their political humour and that simply wasn't Yarwood's thing. It was however perfect for a puppet satire showcase starting fourteen months after this Yarwood show…

"Spitting Image" had quickly evolved from a clunky slow-moving political revue into one of the biggest, most controversial and lucrative comedy hits of the decade. It had taken a lot of money, time and patience to even get it on the air but by the time **"A Non-Denominational Spitting Image Holiday Special"** (10pm, ITV, December 27th 1987) appeared, it seemed to have all be worth it. The previous few years had seen nothing but increased success with an American adaptation for NBC and even a No.1 hit single spoofing inane holiday records titled "The Chicken Song", with lyrics from head writers Rob Grant and Doug Naylor, both of whom had since decided to leave the programme in order to work some sci-fi sitcom or other. For the remaining writing staff - headed by Ian Hislop and Nick Newman with future "Absolutely" men John (soon to be Jack) Docherty and Moray Hunter - there was still much to be angry about in 1987; a magnificent Election special aired that June, immediately after the exit polls captured the hopelessness many felt at five more years of Thatcher.

This less topical but no more polite festive episode was the second one-off of the year and, if it doesn't quite scale the same heights, there are some great laughs nonetheless. Geoffrey Howe bores a filing cabinet at the Tory office party; a Fleet Street hack reworks the birth of Christ for the papers (*"Virgin in No Sex Baby Sensation! God Named In Baby Riddle Scandal"*); a desperate advert with a laugh in its voice nails the dire nature of Pantomimes (*"Cinderella, there'll be no more testicles for you!"*, *"Its 'balls', isn't it?"*, *"It certainly is!"*) and lots more music[45] with a spoof of Chas 'N' Dave's jaunty adverts for Courage Best Bitter becoming "Let's Go Drinking and Driving" (*"and put innocent lives at r-i-i-i-sk...."*) Elsewhere, Perry Como is dreaming of a TV special just like the ones he

---

[45] Although sadly nothing as good as 1986's "Santa Claus is on the Dole", a minor hit released as a follow up to "The Chicken Song" the previous November.

used to get (*"When sleigh bells jingle / I release another single / for both of my fans who aren't dead yet"*) and Bruce Springsteen generally bums everyone out. There's also animation with the careless and disinterested "Temporary Postman Pratt" (*"and his student over-draft"*) and, in the episode's funniest moment, an unsurprisingly much shorter sequel to Raymond Briggs' classic with "The Snowman in The Kalahari". There is crap dated jokes about Michael Jackson dreaming of "a white Christmas" under the surgeon's knife and Rudolf's nose glowing due to being near the Sellafield nuclear site but they move along so fast it's hard to be bored.

It was brash, loud and looked quite cheap - the exact reverse of ITV's earlier spectaculars starring the hugely talented Stanley Baxter who'd made his name with high budget performances and note-perfect Hollywood spoofs in which he would play every part. Sadly, these were not the times for being expensive and he was let go leading to a much-publicised return to his original home on the BBC. Sadly, the magic was hard to recreate and **"Stanley Baxter's Picture Annual"** (9:30pm, BBC One, December 29th 1986) would be his last programme for some time. It's a nice if not especially side-splitting send-off though with a Western spoof featuring Noel Coward as the Sheriff and The Queen opening the new season on TV (*"There will be dramatic cutbacks. Open All Hours will have to close at 5, Dallas will be replaced by Bishop's Stortford..."*) are the highlights. You can't keep a good nonagenarian down though and Baxter would return first to Channel 4 for two new programmes in the mid-90s then back to ITV for the festive tribute "Now and Then" on Christmas Day 2008 and yet another in 2019, this time for Channel Five. Baxter would also return to the BBC for two long-running series on Radio Four – the detective comic drama "Two Pipe Problems" with Richard Briars and "The Stanley Baxter Playhouse", a series of comic playlets.

Also jumping from ITV back to Auntie Beeb after a few minor disagreements with their radio department, **"The Kenny Everett Television Show"** (7:45pm, BBC One, December 24th 1981) was a perfect calling card beginning with spinning newspapers revealing his defection (*"Biggest betrayal since Pearl Harbour!" – Daily Mail, "Who Cares?" – Gay News*) followed by some black and white faux-horror movie footage of Everett being bundled out of a car marked "ITV1" and buried in a shallow grave before being dug up again by two BBC chaps in a clapped-out Austin. With this, Everett fired warning shots at both sides AND mocked his own place in the showbusiness world – and all in the first 40 seconds! Much like his previous Thames shows there are cut-out animations, familiar characters, a set full of television screens and no studio audience yet but bags of confidence from the get go. Plus, it's very, very funny. A memorable running sketch finds Ken wandering the corridors of the much-missed BBC TV Centre explaining what all the initials on the doors mean ("DG: Director General", "OB OPS: Outside Broadcast Operators"). He then assumes "BUM" must naturally stand for "Broadcasting Under Manager" but is instead, terrifically, a giant bottom which later blasts Terry Wogan through a nearby wall.

At the time, Wogan was probably best known as the host of comedy panel game "Blankety Blank" which regularly made appearances on Christmas Day including one episode in 1983 featuring the contestant Captain Tom Moore who would become a household name in 2020 thanks to his huge NHS fundraising efforts aged 99. It would also be noteworthy as Wogan's final episode as host of the long-running series. Replacing him would be a man who'd never presented a game show before but possessed one of the greatest comic minds with a mixture of wordplay and character-work that wasn't given nearly enough credit in his lifetime. Les Dawson had made his name on the other side with Yorkshire TV's panel show "Joker's Wild" and his own long-running "Sez Les" (11 series between 1969 and 1976) before he moved to the BBC for **"The Dawson Watch"**. This had Les embracing the (relatively) modern age with a spoof consumer programme backdrop for his sketches. Each episode had a theme and the topic on the December 23rd 1980 was unsurprisingly "Christmas" (8:30pm) with a two-hander in a toy shop perhaps the standout moment: *"I've never forgotten the set of wooden building blocks that my uncle bought me when I was a small boy. They certainly broadened my mind."*

"Oh how?"

"I use them to stand on to look into next door's bedroom window."

There's also Les as the titular skinflint in the traditional Scrooge parody and of course, the gossiping Cissie (Roy Barraclough) and Ada (Dawson) are on hand to discuss the season. Over three series, he worked with newer writers such as Andy Hamilton and Terry Ravenscroft, firmly re-establishing Dawson as one of the top comics of the day. *"Sorry about that, ladies and gentlemen, we've got what is known in TV circles as a temporary technical disparity on the cybernetic audio / visual interface...in other words, a cock-up!"*

It was a unique sense of humour that few managed to nail better than Les' fellow Lancastrian Victoria Wood who had also broken through on a TV talent show (Les on "Opportunity Knocks" in 1967, Victoria on "New Faces" in 1974.) By the time the pilot **"Wood and Walters – Two Creatures Great and Small"** (10:20pm, ITV, January 1st 1981) was made, she'd already been on several dodgy shows as well as singing topical songs for "That's Life". After working with Julie Walters in a serious revue entitled "In at The Death", she wrote the play "Talent" which would quickly be picked up for TV by Granada Television's legendary producer Peter Eckersley. A sequel followed in 1980 – "Nearly a Happy Ending" – before the offer of a sketch show came in. Not feeling confident enough to front it alone, Julie Walters was drafted in for a fun half hour of songs, monologues and comedy bits that already fizzed with Wood's trademark character wordplay (*"I couldn't get steamed up about intercourse one way or the other. Oh, I do it y'know, don't get me wrong but I don't smile or nuttin"*) Eckersley's tragic early death before a full series could be made left Wood distraught and with no desire to continue.

Eventually one series emerged, beginning exactly a year later on 1st January 1982. Despite the circumstances in which it was made there's a lot of strong material throughout and it's a signpost towards the amazing work that would follow when she moved to BBC Two for the sublime "Victoria Wood - As Seen on TV". These were so successful BBC One quickly repeated them for a wider audience and after a series of playlets for the channel was given her first Christmas Day programme **"Victoria Wood's All Day Breakfast"** (9pm, BBC One, December 25th 1992) which mercilessly parodied the daytime magazine format of shows like ITV's "This Morning", fronted at that point by married couple Richard Madeley and Judy Finnegan. Here, we get partners Martin Cumbernauld (Duncan Preston) and Sally Crossthwaite (Wood herself) cropping up throughout the 50 minutes with Martin felling "no embarrassment at all" discussing "female problems" like "wonky wombs and faulty fallopian tubes". Between the links are regular visits to "The Mall" which did for the BBCs new soap flop "Eldorado" what Wood's earlier "Acorn Antiques" had for "Crossroads" with a predictable but fun connection to Wood's earlier work in the final act. There's also and a short interview with old friend and special guest Alan "Dickman" Rickman which is tear-inducingly funny. **"Victoria Wood: Live in Your Own Home"** came next on Christmas Day 1994 with Wood performing solo stand-up, songs and new character monologues from her recent UK tour to 13.69m delighted homes. Perhaps best of the lot was **"Victoria Wood with All the Trimmings"** (9:15pm, BBC One, December 25th 2000) which manages satirise the changing state of TV through a range of different genres and backed with her starriest cast to date.

Also coming via BBC Two to Christmas Day on BBC One would be French and Saunders, sometimes separately in "The Vicar of Dibley" or "Absolutely Fabulous" and occasionally together. To anyone hearing their earliest material which was so strong even Channel 4 had to move their first TV half hour post-11pm due to the sexual nature of the content[46], Dawn and Jennifer being beloved enough to get a slot on one of the most family friendly telly days of the year might be a

---

[46] In particular the use of the word "clitoris". I apologise if this has similarly caused you great upset to read.

surprise. But that is the beauty of their act which is very naughty and very silly but made by two incredibly talented performers who always manage to bring something interesting to whatever they do. The **"French & Saunders Christmas Special"** (9pm, BBC Two, December 28th 1988) was the first of seven festive shows they would make for the BBC to date and is full of great moments including the series' most controversial sketch to date with Jim and Jim – the comedians done up with fat suits to play dirty old men – paying "tribute" to the Queen. (*"Queen or no Queen – she's got wimmin's needs!"*) The piece led to complaints and the Tory MP Anthony-Beaumont-Dark demanded that an inquiry should be made in that way Tory MPs generally do. The centrepiece is a terrific spoof of Bananarama as Paula Yates attempts to interview pop sensations Lananeeneenoonoo, with Kathy Burke as third member Kim. Their next big special wouldn't be for another six years although it would herald their first new show on BBC One where the wonderful "Celebrity Christmas Puddings" in 2002 and 2017's semi-retrospective "300 Years of French and Saunders" would appear on the 25th.

A similar double act route, minus a Christmas Day show sadly, was that of Mel Smith and Griff Rhys-Jones who would spend the nineties on BBC One after four series of the brilliant "Alas Smith and Jones". This had been one of the most popular sketch shows of the eighties and **"Smith and Jones - The Home-Made Xmas Video"** (9:30pm, BBC Two, December 23rd 1987) expanded on some characters first seen in that series. A British working-class family seen via the new-fangled home camcorder, there's well-meaning but quick to temper Dad (Jones), happy but put-upon Mum (Diane

Langton), kids Shirley and Peter (Jenny Jay and Nigel Harman) and their fun, illiterate and frequently drunk lodger Len (Smith) who almost anticipates the character of Homer Simpson. Sequences involving simple acts like putting a wreath on the door, badly stealing a tree and visiting sick relatives are made into painfully funny moments that are never played cheaply for cringe laughs. Likewise, the family are rough but never sneered at by Griff and Robin Driscoll's affectionate but honest script which makes them fully rounded likeable characters who could easily have been spun off into a full series. The show is also of note for being one of the first made by Mel and Griff's new independent production house TalkBack which would soon become a very big deal in British comedy.

"Alas Sage and Onion" (9pm. BBC Two, December 21st 1988) was to be Mel and Griff's swansong for the channel that made their name but is undoubtedly one of their very strongest shows with a deconstruction of the Morecambe and Wise act, a head-to-head chat about New Year's resolutions and the sight of Smith trying to dispose of an unwanted gift giraffe over a bridge amongst the stand outs. It also unfortunately had the bad fortune to follow a newsflash reporting the Lockerbie disaster in which a bomb on a Pan-Am jet enroute from London to New York exploded causing a crash into a small Scottish town. A sketch about air traffic controllers was apparently excised minutes before it went to air but whether viewers were ready for the sight of Smith and Jones hanging from tinsel nooses in the opening sequence is another matter. Certainly, the usual biting and occasionally taste-pushing tone of their regular shows remained with the game show spoof "Bigotry" savaging Rupert Murdoch and the gutter press, a gunman accidentally bringing down The

Snowman mid-flight and the Police watching graphic bloody crime scene videos at their Christmas party. The finale is a beautifully filmed Martin Scorsese sendup as the nativity gets the guns 'n' grittiness take in "The First Temptation of Christ" before a holiday sweater-wearing Mel and Griff talk us through their Christmas plans and wish us – and inevitably, BBC Two - goodbye: *"If you enjoyed watching it half as much as we enjoyed making it, well then I'm sorry you had such a lousy time..."*

A double act unusually going to opposite way featured in the pilot of **"A Bit of Fry and Laurie"** (11:55pm, BBC One, December 26th 1987) later to become one of BBC Two's best comedy programmes. Despite its rather ridiculous timeslot, this terrific introduction sets out Stephen and Hugh's already well-honed act admirably with many of the themes that would become synonymous with the pair courtesy of a gallery of buffoons, bores and bloody! business! men! Highlights include the self-explanatory "Privatisation of the Police Force" which is then dismantled by duelling arts shows, Hugh's exquisite jazz ballad "Mystery" about an increasingly unlikely romance (*"Taken a violent dislike to me / I'd be foolish to ignore the possibilities / That if we had ever actually met / you might have hated me / Still, that's not the only problem that I can see / Dead since 1973..."*) and a suitably over-the-top parody of convoluted Australian soap opera plots (*"You mean we've been sleeping together all this time...behind my back?"*)

Also coming to BBC Two via Channel 4's "Saturday Live" was Harry Enfield who'd hit big with his kebab shop character Stavros in early 1986 before going stratospheric with Loadsamoney who chimed perfectly with the

Thatcherite privatised era of greed. When Enfield was signed up for his own BBC Two sketch series it was perhaps a surprise to many that he would ditch these older characters in favour of a whole new cast of grotesques and idiots. **"Harry Enfield's Festive Television Programme"** (9:20pm, BBC Two, December 24th 1992) found him joined by Paul Whitehouse as the miserable Old Gits running a "Santa's Grotty". Both also played dumb and dumber workmen Lee and Lance discussing the point of The Queen and whether she should be replaced by Bob Monkhouse. Their best is saved for last however when insincere, self-obsessed DJs Smashie and Nicey take to a hospital as they do a lot of great work for charity but don't like to "sing about it" before performing a magnificent and self-aggrandizing overblown ballad (*"I can't walk past a / natural disaster / no-one's there faster / with signed photographs / I turn up quite 'liderally' / at every catastrophe / I've saved humanity / on your behalf".*) This would be last of thirteen programmes made for BBC Two after being poached by the parent channel for "Harry Enfield and Chums". It's a perfect end to one of the great sketch shows that people still quote even 25 years on. As Dave Nice might say, *"Bum tiddle tiddle bum tiddle tiddle bum bum bum bum."*

Much like Enfield, Rory Bremner had also started his career with impressions and for a time was probably the only person working in his genre anyone could name. **"Rory Bremner... and the Morning After the Year Before"** (10pm, Channel 4, January 1st 1993) kicked off what would turn into 17 years at Channel 4 after seven series at the BBC and countless appearances on everything from Radio 4's satirical revue "WeekEnding" to the Jimmy Cricket's ITV sketch show "And

There's More". The last of his BBC shows was barely six months old when he was popped up here with a satirical look back at the previous year. A hugely talented impersonator, Bremner had slowly added a more political side to his work as he'd gone on even if he wasn't quite ready to let go of the likes of Roger Moore, Denis Norden, Michael Fish, Geoff Boycott, Harry Carpenter, Barry Norman and Ronnie Corbett just yet, preferring to weave them into a more topical script with Bob Monkhouse for example used here to ask which MPs have actually read the Maastricht Treaty.

Definitely a show for the more discerning, perhaps older viewer, the framing device of a cloudy John Major watching a programme from the previous night to remind himself of 1992 is a smart one as is the fake continuity announcement *"some more smart-arsed satire from the bloke we pinched from the BBC"*. Befitting the year just passed, there are jokes about Benetton, Sinead O'Connor ripping up a photo of the Pope, Paddy 'Pantsdown', the Queen in a smoking Windsor Castle, "don't you just love being in control?", Nigel Mansell being boring, Right Said Fred, Sky stealing the football coverage, Bill Clinton "not inhaling", Madonna's "Sex" book and more with only some brownface for a Trevor McDonald impersonation feeling a real misstep. Sadly, despite them being part of his later BBC series, John Bird and John Fortune are not featured here but would soon reappear later that year in "Rory Bremner, Who Else?" and the more egalitarian follow-up series "Bremner, Bird and Fortune". Ultimately, it's an interesting nostalgia trip, not exactly railing at any single party or getting angry in any way, merely pointing out the mistakes that were made along the way. In the current climate, it makes me unsurprisingly nostalgic for a time where misbehaving MPs apologised or even stepped down from power. Sigh.

"And now it's time for a few of my Rory Bremner impressions..."

Imagine never having seen an episode of Harry Hill's very cult sketch series and being greeted by the sight of an elderly actor on top of a tree declaring himself *"the self-styled fairy king of Yule"*. That was Barrie Gosney and this is **"Harry Hill's Christmas Sleigh Ride"** (10:30pm, Channel 4, December 23rd 1998) where viewers are plunged straight into a Cliff Richard medley before an opening stand-up routine followed by clarinettist Acker Bilk playing Christmas carols on the comb and paper. It's a mystifying start if you're not familiar with the running jokes but for those of us who watched avidly every week, this was the sild on the cake.

Bringing us back round to many of the names we've already seen in this chapter, Hill's Channel 4 series felt like a 1970s Saturday night variety show that slipped through a time warp with the celebrity guests swapped out for a series of odd characters like Ken Ford: the man "from the Joy of Sex books", Harry's stun-gun wielding mother and the actor Bert Kwouk who is employed as an incompetent chicken catcher. There are also traces of "The Goodies" in sections like the strange mini-sitcom "Harry and Burt at Home" presenting the Rory McGrath-obsessed lives of Hill and Kwouk who this week dress up as Mulder and Scully to question how Santa gets round the entire world in one night. Burt would rather catalogue his "Guns of Navarone" collection (*"they're all the same!" "Oh yeah, why would they show the same movie every year?"*) but Harry proposes trapping a Santa in a wheelie bin for his gifts. This again makes it feel like a series from a different era but with a very modern Dadaist twist and nothing represents that more than Ted Rogers suddenly appearing to do a "3-2-1" clue which results in Harry turning down his dream prize - some Sild. You know, sild - the canned young herring, invariably in a sauce. Siiiiiiiiiiilllld.

"You know what us cats like to do at Christmas.....SIT ON A BABY'S FACE" Ah, at least we have Stouffer the Cat, Harry's blue puppet pet who is joined by a similarly operated Baby Jesus for a talk. Babies in general are high on the agenda this episode as Hill's Abbey National book-obsessed wife gives birth to a baby that looks suspiciously like Ken Ford before the whole cast sing "I Wish It Could Be Christmas Everyday" dressed as babies for.... reasons.

One of those programmes it's impossible to make people like if they don't get it, this wouldn't have the broader appeal of "TV Burp" or the equally daft "Alien Fun Capsule" but, like Harry Enfield, Vic and Bob or even "Monty Python's Flying Circus" before him, Hill created a world that ran on his own rules and logic and anyone brave enough to step inside was in for a sorted time. Respect due.

Muppetational Moments

As keen trousered readers will have hopefully noticed, the film section running throughout this very book is named after the spectacular song which opens 1981's **"The Great Muppet Caper"**. It definitely fits as not only did every Muppet film bar one (ironically "The Great Muppet Caper") first appeared on television around Christmas time with three – 1979's **"The Muppet Movie"**, the flawless **"The Muppet Christmas Carol"** (1992) and the underrated **"Muppets in Space"** (1999) – being shown on Christmas Day in 1981, 1997 and 2003 respectively[47]. There's just something festive about Kermit and his pals that TV seems to love.

Their first appearance in this country billed as "the Muppets" aired on Christmas Eve 1973 with actors Joey Heatherton and Art Carney[48] in **"The Perry Como Winter Show"**. First broadcast the previous December in the US, the smooth crooner Como brought Jim Henson, Frank Oz and Jerry Juhl along to provide some colour to a loose story about travelling through Vermont at Christmastime. None of the more

---

[47] "The Muppets Take Manhattan" bowed on December 16th 1990, "Muppet Treasure Island" was first broadcast on December 28th 1999, not half bad TV production "It's a Very Merry Muppet Christmas Movie" (2002) was New Year's Eve 2003, excellent reboot "The Muppets" (2011) deserved Christmas Day but got December 29th 2014 and its sequel "Muppets Most Wanted" (2014), only mildly ruined by Ricky Gervais filled the afternoon of December 28th 2016. Even Henson's non-Muppet movies "The Dark Crystal" (1982) and "Labyrinth" (1986) first appeared – albeit the wrong way round chronologically - on December 27th 1990 and Christmas Eve 1989.

[48] Who'd already become acquainted with the gang after appearing in Henson's special "The Great Santa Claus Switch" in 1970 and would later make an appearance in "The Muppets Take Manhattan". Como too had worked with Henson who guested on a 1965 edition of "Perry Como's Kraft Music Hall".

recognisable characters are on show however with the hillbilly guitar plucking 'The Country Trio' the most recognisable from episodes of the Henson's first major series later in the decade, not to mention being caricatures of their real-life puppeteers Henson, Oz and Juhl.

That series was of course **"The Muppet Show"** which would make the characters household names would first appear on British television in September 1976 via media giant Lord Lew Grade's ATV franchise of ITV. It was an instant hit and, even if not specifically made for the Christmas market, episodes starring Julie Andrews and Danny Kaye – neither a stranger to our screens at the festive period – would take pride of place in the middle of the commercial broadcaster's schedule on December 25th 1977 and 1978. Liza Minelli on December 28th 1979 and Marty Feldman on December 21st 1980 would follow with the comedian, fresh off the production of his now forgotten religious satire "In God We Tru$t", joined by the Sesame Street cast for a bit of channel-hopping fun with the googly-eyed Cookie Monster meeting his biggest fan in the host.

As the show wrapped up its fifth season and Henson reverted his gaze to the big screen a fascinating if slightly disquieting look behind the scenes of the British-produced series aired as **"Of Muppets and Men"** (5pm, ITV, December 27th 1981) This feeling of unease stems slightly from Henson and Co's openness to show the full process of puppeteering which takes a little of the magic out of proceedings as we see our felt friends being man-handled (or should that be Muppet-handled?) on quite stark film which is in contrast to the incorporated clips from the very colourful video-based series. It's to the original show's credit though that the audience never thinks of all the hard work that goes into making everything flow when watching Kermit and friends do their thing. The multi-tasking skills by Oz, Richard Hunt, Jerry Nelson, Kathryn Mullen and others are truly amazing to see and comedy fans will love seeing the writer's meetings with Henson and Oz riffing in character. Later a scene with British puppet legend Louise Gold, Steve Whitmire and Dave Goelz trying to sing during attempts at gargling is pure joy. An essential document of an amazing series.

Even though "The Muppet Show" itself never went all out on Christmas, the special **"John Denver and The Muppets - A Christmas Together"** (8:10pm, BBC One, December 15th 1979) certainly did. Broadcast by "the other side" just ten days after its American debut, it's a much more sedate and soppy affair than the Muppets' own programmes[49] with a mixture of original and traditional seasonal songs that would get a simultaneous release on RCA Records. Sketches featuring the Muppets working on the script (*"Peace on Earth, Goodwill to all men and women and chickens and bears...and Dizzy Gillespie!"*) and staging songs are great fun as always but Denver is not an engaging presence at all. Still, Rowlf the Dog gets his own song which is always a winner in this house. The two groups would reconvene again in 1983 for the camping themed "Rocky Mountain Holiday" although a flying sequence has since been removed for modern audience due to you know...John Denver and everything.

---

[49] Country folk singer Denver had already guested on an episode of "The Muppet Show" that year and clearly it had been an enjoyable experience for all. That episode would been seen by most of the UK on December 14th 1979, one day before this broadcast.

Also singing and dancing were the characters in Henson's earlier special **"Emmet Otter's Jug-Band Christmas"** (3:15pm, ITV, December 24th 1978) based on Russell Hoban's 1971 children's tale of the same name. Introduced by Kermit the Frog,[50] "Emmet" is a beautiful, touching, funny, ridiculous and full of terrific new Paul Williams songs and perfect for giving you the warm fuzzies...which is apt for when you're watching a bunch of warm fuzzies, I suppose. Emmet and his mother Alice live an honest but poor life in an old shack barely getting by doing odd jobs until each of them notices that a big prize talent contest is happening and decides to surprise the other by entering. Originally shown by HBO in December 1977, its quaint but funny. There's a more anarchic side too when their town is over-run by teenage menaces who later form – with a hat-tip to Alice Cooper – the glam rocking Riverbottom Nightmare Band.

Also living in the "Muppets but not Those Muppets" category was "Fraggle Rock". Created with no less of a goal then to teach love and peace to the world the Fraggles were cute, underground creatures that learnt lessons, sang songs and undeniably taught viewers about love and peace. Above them lived a number of human counterparts (or the Silly Creatures of Outer Space as the fuzzy favourites know them) depending on where in the world you were watching. The overall show stayed the same but with a nice local touch on the outside. So, in the US the Fraggles would live undetected below a workshop owned by kindly inventor Doc and his puppet dog Sprocket while over in France it was a former

---

50   Unless you're watching the Region 2 DVD release from 2011 where the bits with Kermit setting the story up are completely snipped out for some reason. He was returned for the 40th anniversary edition.

bakery with chef Doc and his dog Croquette. The UK had The Captain, played by a post- "Porridge" Fulton Mackay, and Sprocket living in a lighthouse and this is how its best remembered by British kids. Sadly, rights issues have kept most of these English versions from being repeated or released on video but a few do exist on YouTube from private collections.

"The Bells of Fraggle Rock" (9:25am, ITV, December 22nd 1984) would be the series' only festive special although festivities are the last thing on wannabe adventurer Gobo's mind as he dismisses the Fraggles' own Solstice holiday, the Festival of the Bells, as a waste of time. He decides to follow an old map to find a bell at the centre of the titular rock but all is not as it seems. A brief scene of the Fraggles frozen solid is really quite eerie but as an analogy for losing belief as you get older and the truth not being as important as happiness (or not freezing to death), it's a beautiful story. The original song sung at the festival is gorgeous too, all full of trumpets and harmonies, the sort of thing Henson productions did so well. The Fraggles would appear again in 1987's delightful one-off **"A Muppet Family Christmas"** (8:30am, BBC One, December 26th 1989) when Kermit and Robin accidentally stumble upon the entrance to their secret world and share a song.

The whole special is a joy too with Kermit and all the gang (and I mean ALL – Sesame Street, Muppet Babies, even Jim Henson himself) descending on an unsuspecting Fozzie's mum who was just heading out the door to Malibu. A collection of sketches under one roof, the only real plotline is Miss Piggy's attempts to make it through the snow and reach the others after running late at a photoshoot. It's especially lovely to see characters from different presentations interact and there are plenty of songs as you'd expect from the Muppets like The Electric Mayhem bashing through "Jingle Bell Rock".

It's such a great hour of entertainment that it's a shame it was relegated to an early morning slot here when America had made it a prime-time programme for all the family. Since his passing in May 1990, much of Henson's work seems to be disregarded as just for kids in the UK which is a huge shame considering the constant attempts he made to innovate and experiment in projects like the 1982 dark fantasy film "The Dark Crystal" or the later NBC anthology series "The Jim Henson Hour" which mixed both the traditional characters with new stories and animation techniques. Although no British channel would air the series in full, various chunks would land on Channel 4's doorstep such as the dark folk tales introduced by John Hurt as "The StoryTeller" and **"Living with Dinosaurs"**[51] (5:50pm, Channel 4, December 30th 1990) which despite the title had nothing to do with the sitcom "Dinosaurs" although both were produced by Henson's company.

For a programme worked on written by future Oscar winner Anthony Minghella, directed by Paul Weiland, produced by Duncan Kenworthy and starring Juliet Stevenson you'd think more people would have heard of this sentimental one-off story about a socially isolated young boy and his toy dinosaur. This might be in part to it being co-produced by TVS Films – a branch of the ITV region Television South who had

---

[51] "Living With Dinosaurs" was earmarked for "The Jim Henson Hour" after its British debut but would be cancelled before it did and later aired on Nickelodeon in the States as a standalone film.

previously had a hand in bringing the Fraggles to the screen. After TVS lost their licence in 1992, their output came to be owned, via a complicated series of mergers and buyouts, by Disney. "Living with Dinosaurs" is a well-written if slightly downbeat show but very representative of the boundaries Jim Henson was trying to push, right up until his tragically early death.

The fact the Muppet franchise not only continued but didn't collapse entirely over the Disney take over is testament to the talent behind the scenes. The fact that anyone still knows them sixty years on - thirty years since the death of the person at the very top too - is impressive with 1992's "The Muppet Christmas Carol" now a yearly staple for millions. When Disney+ announced "The Muppet Show" was going to be added to the platform in February 2021 the internet practically exploded with delight as it's still a series full of laughs, music and genuine heart which will always carry Henson's legacy through any highs, lows and wonky voiced Kermits that might follow. And if that isn't the spirit of Christmas, I don't know what is!

Hey! A Movie! The Nineties

1990

As a new decade bowed, it was time to look to the future and perhaps even…the stars. And so, BBC One greeted the first appearance on the box for one of the most iconic characters that simultaneously looked a bit like a tod - **"E.T: The Extra Terrestrial"** - at 3:05pm. Less inspiring was the lacklustre Diane Keaton 1987 comedy **"Baby Boom"** which took up the 9:45pm slot. With 17 and a half million watching the skies for our brown alien chum, ITV decided to play it safe in opposition with the 1979 Bond film **"Moonraker"** (3:05pm) getting its third festive run out in under a decade. The fireworks were put on hold instead for **"Beverly Hills Cop II"** (8pm) which saw over 12 and a half million settle down for another 'specially ruined for television' adventure with Axel Foley.

On variety alone, BBC Two undeniably won out with the first TV broadcast of Claude Berri's two-part saga **"Jean De Florette"** (8:20pm) with "Manon des Sources" following on Boxing Day. Plus, the sequel to the experimental, dialogue free documentary "Koyaanisqatsi", 1988's **"Powaqqatsi"** (3:50pm) and horrendous child-scarring animation **"Watership Down"** (9:30am) all sharing space. Over on Channel 4 there's a selection of WC Fields classics including **"It's A Gift"** (3:30pm) on Christmas afternoon and at night 1988's fantasy drama "Rouge" (12:15am) continued a "Chinese Ghost Stories" strand.

Fans of men in barely knacker-covering animal furs could also thrill to a season of Tarzan movies each morning on BBC Two with the then-four years dead Johnny Weissmuller in the title role. And BBC One bigged up their acquisition of the brown bab-looking thing from space with a season of Spielberg movies. "ET, Phone 081 811 8181" …

1991

A stunningly dark film for all the family at tinsel-topped tea time (body count: 56), Tim Burton's 1989 reimagining of **"Batman"** appears at 6pm on BBC One despite famous being the movie that ushered in the 12 Certificate for cinemas here in Britain. Being nine at the time of its release in 1989 I can remember being geed up to bursting point thanks to all the merchandising – much of it aimed at kids – including Prince's soundtrack but had to wait until an irresponsible cousin let me watch it on video the year after. When it came to the terrestrial TV premiere, it was just as big a deal for BBC One too who even made a special variant on its then-current globe logo which thrillingly became lit up by a giant bat signal. Sadly, it didn't get much more use as ITV snapped up the rights to show all the sequels from "Batman Returns" onwards. At least they had the good sense to save Eddie Murphy's raucous comedy **"Coming to America"** (9:30pm) until later in the evening followed by the unsurprisingly austere finale to **"The Likely Lads"** (11:55pm) saga.

ITV's week was oddly muted with more old favourites and ropey TV movies than new releases BUT as well as some diminishing Christmas Day returns for **"Crocodile Dundee II"** (8pm) which wouldn't even make the top twenty for the week there is room for two - TWO! - "Police Academy" premieres with 1987's **"Citizens on Patrol"** (11:15pm) on

Christmas night and the following year's **"Assignment Miami Beach"** three days later. What a time to be alive!

A surprisingly quiet day film-wise for Channel 4 too with just Hitchcock's 1954 mystery favourite **"Dial M For Murder"** at 12:10am. Boxing Day onwards however would find a place for a string of Jackie Chan films just as he was starting to make a name for himself outside of Hong Kong cinema.

And for fans of French cinema, how about three of the buggers, as subtitled as you please, on BBC Two, with the TV debut of Ingrid Bergman in Jean Renoir's 1956 romantic comedy **"Elena et les hommes"** (11:45am) and to sweeten the deal – two black and white numbers from director Jean Vigo - **"Zéro de Conduite"** (10:20pm) from 1933 and the following year's **"L'Atalante"** (11pm). Plus, a 1939 American obscurity in the middle called **"The Wizard of Oz"** (3:10pm) which by this point had been part of Christmas week ten times since its premiere in 1975.

1992

More whip whapping fun in the day's top-rated film **"Indiana Jones and The Last Crusade"** (3:10pm) with 15.80 million viewers seeing how the trilogy ended. And it did end. There was no fourth film. No. Willy Russell's wonderful 1989 comedy **"Shirley Valentine"** (9:50pm) eased out Christmas night to the delight of 13.86 million viewers although viewers buzzing off too many sprout and eggnog Pop Tarts could stay up for Chuck Heston in 1974's ridiculous **"Earthquake"** at 11:40pm. BBC Two's Christmas weekend seemed very familiar from previous years bar a high quality first showing on network TV for Stephen Frears' saucy period drama **"Dangerous Liaisons"** (9pm) along with **"Rear Window"** (11:50pm) heralding another Hitchcock season.

With so many great choices its little surprise that ITV more or less threw in the towel before they'd even started with a repeat showing of **"Supergirl"** (3:05pm) followed later by a mystifying double bill of the average Martin Short and Nick Nolte comedy crime vehicle **"Three Fugitives"** (7:50pm) and the long-forgotten 1986 ice hockey drama **"Youngblood"** (10pm) which probably made the cut due to starring a pre-superstar Rob Lowe and Patrick Swayze. Channel Four seemed to make little effort too again with Chuck Jones' part-animated psychedelic whimsy **"The Phantom Tollbooth"** (3pm) and 1990's Derek Jacobi-headlining Victorian satire **"The Fool"** (8:40pm). Also making an appearance late at night from Christmas Day onwards are a number of films by Jacobi's equal cinematic legend Godzilla starting with **"Son of Godzilla"** (1am) described by my friend Garreth, an expert on these things thusly *"The Godzilla suit is, erm, an interesting design... But it has solid enemies and an interesting sci-fi plot, in amongst the rompily-soundtracked giant reptile parenting sequences. A game of two halves, then!"*

1993

This was a year where BBC One dominated the ratings so much that ITV hadn't just thrown in the towel this time but acquired controlling shares in the towel industry. This victory had been helped along by the odd partnership of **"Back to The Future Part III"** (4:05pm) and **"Ghost"** (9:10pm) with the latter managing to freak out over 18 million viewers thanks to that creepy bit with the falling glass pane at the end.

On Two, viewers could find a whopping seven films including the very different classics **"The Railway Children"** (12:40pm) and **"Belle de Jour"** (10:55pm). Only one was new though - Michael Palin's pleasant **"American Friends"** (7:30pm) based on the life of his great grandfather. Lots of obscurities over on Four as part of a "Christmas In New York" theme week with Jonathan Demme's **"Cousin Bobby"** (7:30pm) and a short Kenneth Branagh directed adaptation of Chekhov's **"Swan Song"** (8:30pm) featuring John Gielgud and Richard Briars. Late night **"Monkey Business"** (12:50pm) on Christmas Day launched another always appreciated Marx Brothers season.

So, what *DID* ITV have then? Well, movies, movies and yet more movies! Starting with **"The NeverEnding Story"** at 3:05pm before a break for some Beadle. Then its **"National Lampoon's Christmas Vacation"** at 6pm followed almost immediately by fantasy drama **"Field of Dreams"** (8pm) and thriller **"DOA"** (9:55pm) Here the problem wasn't so much the lack of options but the fact the movies picked were so utterly middling ones like you'd pass regularly on trips to the video shop without a second look. Bond fans would at least have the terrestrial premiere of **"Licence to Kill"** (1989) to look forward to although not until 3rd January 1994. Until then it was just the regular dog and fish licences…

1994

It's a fairly bare cupboard at ITV Towers again with the dire 1986 Goldie Hawn comedy **"Wildcats"** (8:05pm) slung out in prime-time on Christmas Eve but a Disney double-bill of a channel hopping **"Mary Poppins"** (3:10pm) and a debuting **"Sleeping Beauty"** (6:05pm) on the big day itself is much more welcome… unless you're in one the ITV regions that bizarrely decided to swap Mary for the admittedly also wonderful **"The Empire Strikes Back"** instead.

Skipping right past 1990's horrible **"Jetsons: The Movie"** at 11am, your mileage may vary on **"Robin Hood: Prince of Thieves"** (6:45pm) which takes up a large chunk of Christmas night on BBC One, not to mention 14.31 million viewers although some day closing **"Trading Places"** at 11:30pm is always a lovely sight to behold. A strange day over on BBC Two also which for once had nothing cinematic at all between **"Doctor Dolittle"** at 10am and forgettable Demi Moore comedy **"The Butcher's Wife"** over twelve hours later at 10:25pm. The channel's big acquisition of the year - Oliver Stone's three hour **"JFK"** (1991) would take up a whole evening a few days later on the 28th.

Danny Kaye got his own mini season on Channel 4 with **"Hans Christian Andersen"** (12:55pm) and **"The Secret Life of Walter Mitty"** (3:15pm) providing a lovely change of pace on Christmas afternoon. Closing out every night are more "Chinese Ghost Stories" like 'jiangshi' (effectively "vampire-zombie") comedy **"Mr Vampire"** (1:55am) which eagle-eyed viewers will spot is mostly identical to the season they'd run four years earlier. Spooky!

1995

The early 90s were a strange time for film in the UK with low cinema attendances, videos to rent in every corner shop and Sky's movie channels slowly picking up more subscribers on films for their telly premieres. As such Christmas Day 1995 features a bunch of familiar if not especially inspiring Hollywood flicks with disappointing Peter Pan update **"Hook"** (4:30pm) and the probably not at all suitable for the day **"Indecent Proposal"** (10:10pm) sharing space on BBC One. On ITV, nun comedy fun **"Sister Act"** (8pm) is the big Christmas film along with repeat runs of **"Ghostbusters II"** (3:10pm) and **"Herbie Rides Again"** (11:30am) fulfilling the Disney quotient for the day. 1991's dismal infidelity for laughs comedy **"Scenes from A Mall"** slipped in at 11pm, no doubt hoping to capture some of the same ratings magic "Down and Out in Beverly Hills" by the same director Paul Mazursky and its co-star Bette Midler delivered years earlier.

Fans of more cultured and less-slime and nun-based viewing were probably better suited with BBC Two's big film of the day: the epic 150-minute retelling of Chinese history **"Farewell My Concubine"** (10pm) which had won all of the wards when released in 1993. The rest of the day looked pretty familiar though with **"20,000 Leagues Under The Sea"** at the start of the day (8:50am) and "A Night At The Opera" at the end (1:30am) Equally with their brows raised to the skies, Channel 4 have first runs of **"Elenya"** (1:25pm), a 1992 film about the Second World War as seen by a melancholy little girl in Wales…you know, Christmas stuff…and the Pinter-scripted comedy **"Turtle Diary"** (7pm) which appeared as part of their "Beastly Christmas" season which also found space for the mixed bag of "Leon the Pig Farmer", Yorkshire misery classic "Kes", "Tarzan, The Ape Man" and the superb post-apocalyptic black comedy "A Boy and His Dog".

1996

It's all about **"Jurassic Park"** (6:30pm) which despite everyone in the world seeing it at the time still did deservedly huge business for BBC One with 14 and a half million dinofans watching throughout though sadly it wasn't the Director's Cut with extra dinosaurs. As well as another opportunity to follow the yellow brick road at 11:20am, they also ended the night with two films that had premiered on Christmas Day over on the commercial channel – **"Revenge of The Pink Panther"** (12am) and **"Please Sir!"** (1:40am) which especially feels odd considering it was a spin-off from an ITV sitcom. That channel itself went with a rare bit of finery on Christmas night with Anthony Hopkins and Emma Thompson in the class-based period drama **"The Remains of the Day"** (10pm) although the less said about 'incorrect TV menace' **"Dennis"** (5:25pm) earlier in the day the better. Devotees of Christmas film "Die Hard" will also be pleased to know its scheduled...on New Year's Day. Ho Ho...huh?

Classics ahoy on BBC Two with a double bill of Fred Astaire and Ginger Rogers – **"The Barkleys of Broadway"** (6:45am) and **"The Band Wagon"** (8:30am), **"Casablanca"** (3:10pm) and Woody Allen-before-all-that's **"Play It Again Sam"** (12:40am) It was a similar tale over on Channel 4 with Peter Sellers in **"The Battle of the Sexes"** (6:50pm) and

"**Dial M for Murder**" (9pm) again. Both channels had a premiere at 11pm though – BBC Two showing the shouting real estate men drama **"Glengarry Glen Ross"** while Channel 4 had the "hey, the X Files is a popular thing!" TV movie **"Roswell"** which stuck Kyle MacLachlan and Martin Sheen in the middle of a UFO conspiracy. The truth is… probably somewhere else to be honest.

1997

And after fifteen years, we finally get another new channel in the mix. Having launched the previous March and promising a film every night, Channel 5 was quickly declared to be a tacky unfocused service with increasingly terrible movies at 9pm. Not so over Christmas where Anthony "P.S. I am…" Hopkins returned in another gentle biopic **"84 Charing Cross Road"** (1:10pm) and Reece Witherspoon made her respected debut in **"The Man in the Moon"** (9pm.) In fact, you can almost look over the fact that the baffling **"Michael Jackson's Moonwalker"** (4:20pm) is slap bang between the two. Boxing Night upped the stakes with a double bill of **"Gone with The Wind"** and **"The Happy Hooker"** separated only by an episode of sci-fi also-ran "Lexx". Because it was Channel 5 in 1997.

Over on the old firm BBC One had the terrible live-action **"The Flintstones"** (4:10pm) which peddled in through the courtesy of Fred's two feet ahead of the 1994 surprise action comedy hit **"The Mask"** (6:50pm) Both movies would do well for the channel but neither broke past 10 million viewers barrier, a portent of things to come in the following century.

"Willy Wonka and the Chocolate Factory" (11:05am), **"Airplane!"** (11:45pm) and dating agency-based smut **"Carry on Loving"** (1:10am) also appear although sadly not as an increasingly randy triple bill.

BBC Two continued the strong tradition of black and white favourites alongside the highbrow material we've come to expect and probably not watch by this point with first showings for a 1995 adaptation of Puccini's **"Madame Butterfly"** (5:25pm) and French historical drama **"La Reine Margot"** (10:10pm) On the other side of the coin, there's a series of fifties sci-fi films running last thing every night over Christmas with smashing names like **"Terror from The Year 5000"** and **"War of the Colossal Beast"**.

Very few premieres again for ITV as Sky continued to swoop in and grab stuff years before terrestrial got a sniff. Whether they fought over talking dog adventure **"Homeward Bound: The Incredible Journey"** (12:35pm) is undocumented but they did at least hold the trump card still as **"The Muppet Christmas Carol"** (3:10pm) took pride of place against the Bedrock-based boredom on the other side. Speaking of Trump, **"Home Alone 2: Lost In New York"** (7:30pm) struggled to live up to its predecessor. And not just because of the horrible orange-faced git with illusions of grandeur appearing in a cameo within.

To tie in with their 15th birthday celebrations, there's a season of 'Film on Four' premieres throughout Christmas week on Channel 4 although none of them appear on the day itself with **"Dr Dolittle"** (10am) and **"Kind Hearts and Coronets"** (5:30pm) the only full-length films scheduled throughout the day. Fans of biting people and then running away were served by the late night "Blood Lust" season of vampire films with Hammer's **"Dracula - Prince of Darkness"** (11:05pm) starring Christopher Lee and 1970's grubby **"Lust for a Vampire"** (12:45am) seeing out Christmas night with a bang. Or, at the very least, a hearty suck...

1998

La la la! Yes, it's our porcine pal **"Babe"** (7pm) in the prime slot on BBC One with 8.8 million pig pals watching to make it the biggest film of the day. Bringing similar seasonal cheer was the 1994 remake of **"Miracle on 34th Street"** which got its first terrestrial showing at a rather unbefitting 11am. And there's always room for another not very good chapter of the Carry On series though with **"Carry On Girls"** (12:35am) sending viewers to bed with a…well, maybe let's not go there, shall we? Instead let's smarten the joint up with BBC Two who had **"Casablanca"** (3:10pm) again, Trevor Nunn's **"Twelfth Night"** (6:05pm) and a Gary Oldman double bill with two roles based on real people - Beethoven and playwright Joe Orton - in **"Immortal Beloved"** (10:45pm) and the Alan Bennett-scripted **"Prick Up Your Ears"** (12:45am) respectively. Some excellent Chaplin films are always a boon even if they are on at the eye-moistening hour around 6am.

Amazingly for the first time in decades, ITV have just one film on in the entirety of Christmas Day – **"The Godfather Part II"** – and that's not even on until 10:40pm. The rest of the day being made up by extended soaps, a return to the pantomime format written by "Men Behaving Badly" creator Simon Nye, a Spice Girls concert and "Who Wants to Be a Christmas Millionaire?" Perhaps the winner could buy ITV some more films for the next year…

Luckily the remaining terrestrial channels have got movies coming out of their proverbial ears however with Channel 4 showing everything from **"The Great St Trinian's Train Robbery"** (3:10pm) to **"The Omen"** (10:35pm). The 1996 Michael Frayn farce **"Remember Me?"** (9pm) feels a very odd choice for the evening's big draw even if it does have a cast containing most of British comedy including Robert Lindsay, Rik Mayall, Brenda Blethyn and Imelda Staunton. There's more late horror with **"The Fly"** (12:40am) and **"Return of the Fly"** (2:15am) buzzing in for the black and white "Silent Nights, Deadly Nights" season though you'd be better getting up early than going to bed late for some of the timeslots.

And Channel 5 upgrade from a sex offender turning into a robot with the much more wholesome Doris Day in **"Calamity Jane"** (4:05pm), plus the ever-enjoyable Alastair Sim version of **"Scrooge"** (10:50am) although its annoyingly a colourised version here because that's the sort of thing television did back then. The main draw for night owls with their hands down their joggers is the Russ Meyer season featuring many of the sexploitation king's more watchable films including the TV premiere of 1968's **"Vixen"** (11:35pm) which had been a huge success in the US at the time, making its budget back almost sevenfold.

1999

And, as we dangle helplessly over the decade's end, we can see how much things have changed since the sixties with more and more people having satellite television movie channels, while the video shop experienced its final boom.

The story is the same as the previous few years here with a few big family films on BBC One - **"James and The Giant Peach"** (11am) and **"Jumanji"** (4pm) that would already be old hat to modern kids, with a classic– here it was **"The Italian Job"** (11:50pm) at the end of the day. BBC Two ran the usual mix of beloved old chestnuts – **"Harvey"** (6:25am), **"Singin' in the Rain"** (5:10pm) - and worthy premieres – **"Il Postino"** (8:30pm) and HBO's making of "Citizen Kane" biopic **"RKO 281"** (10:15pm) followed by the film itself at 11:45pm. Likewise, a recycle, rinse and repeat for a lot of the films already shown by ITV in previous years with only the probably quite inappropriate **"Ace Ventura: Pet Detective"** (3:10pm) making it into prime-time.

Channel 4 would also stick with the familiar from the sublime – **"Time Bandits"** (11pm) - to the cock awful - **"Tom and Jerry the Movie"** (8am) - with one of their own drama productions **"The Woodlanders"** (5:40pm) in the middle. At least a late-night run of Akira Kurosawa films and some more lesser-known Godzilla spectaculars got the pulse racing a little more as we prepared to exit out of the century.

So, go on Channel 5, I believe in you. You've got the last paragraph of this over-stuffed tinsel trip down telly's cinematic history – what have you got to dazzle the people and take us into a brave new world...?

…the 1969 sex comedy **"Bob and Carol and Ted and Alice"** (10pm) followed by erotic thriller **"Last Call"** at midnight. I mean I like rumpo as much as the next man but it's Christmas, lads. And the millennium. And baby Jesus' birthday. And we're all going to die the second Y2K strikes and the missiles launch at all the computers with blinking date errors on their terminals.

Or does that sound like something out of a movie…?

New Year's Daze

"And now the end is near / but something something / oh god I'm going to be sick into this plant pot." Ah New Year's Eve, either beloved or despised with no permittable middle ground. Looking back over all these old TV listings has made me nostalgic for a time that I don't really remember and probably never actually existed, where people would have family get-togethers, eat haslet sandwiches, roll back the carpet and play the modern tunes of the day on piano such as "Don't Put Your Daughter in a Lead-Lined Container Full of Barium, Mrs Worthington", "The Neville Chamberlain Rag" and "WAP" by Cardi B and Megan Thee Stallion.

Telly's part in all this was often a confusing one. People staying in want to be entertained but most people are going out so don't want to miss anything good, especially before on demand services and even video recorders. Here's my condensed look at how the small screen covered the Buckfast and beer-stained New Years of old...

1946-1963

Ever since 'Itler and his fascist hordes were sent packing, the BBC were ready to party... in respectable clothing and neckwear of course. Having resumed TV broadcasts in June of **1946**, that December 31st became one of the first times television had comfortably lurched past the witching hour as *"Viewers in their homes are invited to take part in the festivities in the Ballroom at Grosvenor House with Charles Adey and Dawn Leslie Strange and Sidney Lipton and his Orchestra"*. Woo! Yeah! Let's drop a tab of rationed Oxo and go snog some wounded airmen! Later years would offer a link up to St. Thomas's Hospital in London and, as soon would become tradition, Glasgow for the Hogmanay celebrations. ITV would be "On the Town" with a few more interesting choices of location and **1956** offered a party from one of the most happening venues of the decade: "The Trocadero Restaurant, London". Don't look for it now though, it shut down in 1965. That same year found the BBC also bravely inching a little further afield as **"Where's There's Life..."** found host and future Tomorrow's World man Raymond Baxter sticking his beak into celebrations everywhere, with piping in Scotland, working men in The Midlands, pilots in Wales, band-leader Ted Heath at the Chelsea Arts Ball, a view from "the Continent" where *"midnight strikes one hour ahead of us in time"*, and most excitingly "A West Indian Party" where newly arrived families *"get together in London for a rhythmic New Year's Eve to the beat of the Trinidad All-Stars Steel Band, the Calypso chants, and the Caribbean Music of Hugh Scotland."*

Into the early minutes of **1959** next for the first New Year's edition of the traditional Scottish variety series **"The White Heather Club"** from the BBC's television studios in Scotland, although purists may be alarmed to note that regular host Andy Stewart was not yet a feature of the programme. All the same there's time for The Joe Gordon Folk Four, The Andrew Macpherson Singers and The Gie Gordons. And viewers may wish to know that Robert Wilson is appearing at the Tivoli, Aberdeen; Jimmy Logan is in "Sinbad the Sailor" at the Alexandra Theatre, Glasgow, and Alistair McHarg is in "Mother Goose" at the King's Theatre, Edinburgh. From there it's fairly traditional Hogmanay scheduling until…

1964-1969

This new-fangled BBC Two saw in its first new year with the grooviest party in town as its regular "The Beat Room" series ran the special **"Beat in The New!"** (11:35am) with Billy J Kramer and The Dakotas, The Merseybeats and PJ Proby just a few of the names who helped the youngsters of the day rock and roll around their 12" black and white Pye television sets. Unfortunately for the pop crazed youngsters rendered nonsensical by our new Beat overloads, ITV also ran the very similarly themed **"The Year Starts Here…So Ready Steady Go!"** (11:05pm) based around their Friday night pop series in direct competition. Quoted in TV World magazine at the time Francis Hitching, editor of musical programmes in London, described it as *"a programme that wasn't really designed to be watched,"* he said. *"We don't care whether they look in or not, so long as their sets are switched on. We hope people once again will use our programme to get their own New Year parties swinging".*

Brave words for a producer of visual programming who also promised *"model girls, pop stars, actors and actresses, boxers, racing drivers"* dancing to the Rolling Stones, the Dave Clark Five, Manfred Mann and Dusty Springfield. It was a popular enough experiment to repeat in 1965 (at the exact time of 10.52pm) with The Animals, Tom Jones, The Kinks, Lulu, The Who and more but due to its cancellation in December 1966 would be replaced with the decidedly less rock n roll **"A Show for Hogmanay"** which continued for the next few years as the young folk presumably roamed the streets looking for "beat".

BBC One's party also stayed in Scotland for the main transition into the New Year but did manage to sneak in a pre-midnight treat for the younger types with **1967**'s confusingly titled "**Suddenly It's 1968**" (10:55pm) hosted by the man of the moment Simon Dee whose twice-weekly "Dee Time" chat show (or "early evening scene") was the place to be seen. Here he was the face of a New Year's Eve Party from "The Talk of the Town in London" with Julie Felix, The Alan Price Set and Roy Hudd. The programme also took a break for **"Seeing in The New Year in Sweden and Italy"** which must have been extremely exciting back then. By the end of **1968** however the obstreperous Dee was down to one show a week and would soon leave the Beeb over money, leaving the path clear for the equally terrible "**Cilla**" (11pm) although the guests were equally mixed with Matt Monro and Billy Cotton, plus The Irving Davies Dancers as standard. Frankie Howerd was on hand though to offer a bit of tittering into next year with a script courtesy of Ray Galton and Alan Simpson who pretty much owned comedy in the 1960s. This was followed by **"Welcome '69"** (at precisely 12:01am), a Jimmy Logan-hosted variety hour from Scotland and not whatever your filthy mind thought of.

Lulu's back again in **1969** but now over on ITV who have got in on the National Scottery with a "**Hogmanay Party**" (11:40pm) and there's shock waves as Andy Stewart has also switched channels after the demise of "The White Heather Club" to celebrate the opening of The Gateway – Scotland's first ever colour television studio. Meanwhile on BBC One we can **"Ring in the New"** ("starring Moira Anderson") at 12:01am after "**Pop Go the 60s!**" (10:35pm) a co-production between the BBC and ZDF in West Germany featuring performances from many of the decade's biggest acts such as The Bachelors, Cliff Richard, Marmalade, Horst Jankowski, Kenny Ball and his Jazzmen, Sandie Shaw, some lot called the Beatles and bloody Lulu again. Filmed at BBC Television Centre, the introductions were done for both countries with Elfi Von Kalckreuth speaking only in German, whilst the English links came via a rotten old sex offender whose name I won't trouble you with but should definitely have fallen into a threshing machine more, the dirty old "fixing" bastard.

A few days before New Year 1969, ITV had also decided to *"examine this last decade through the eyes of a young man whose knowledge and understanding of the world around him was shaped, almost exclusively, by television."* The programme was **"A Child of The Sixties"** (10:15pm, December 27th 1969) and the child was…Gyles Brandreth. No, really it was!

"Gyles Brandreth is an Oxford undergraduate, President of the Union, co-editor of Isis and directed the Oxford University Dramatic Society." (TV Times)

Known by most as either that gaudily jumpered git on TV-am or the old posh chap who never stops talking on "The One Show", Brandreth has lived a fascinating life and his genuinely recommended collection of diaries 'Something Sensational to Read on The Train' bears out some of the incredible things he was involved with including this special which was taped on 15th December at the London Weekend studios.

"I think we have got plenty of variety in the news clips we are showing, everything from the Aberfan disaster to Tommy Steele's

wedding. The real challenge will be to keep the chat with the guests stimulating and to time.", Brandreth recalled. Those guests being historian Lady Longford, TV producer and former president of CBS News Fred Friendly and the MPs Iain Macleod and Michael Foot of Conservative and Labour respectively. After the broadcast, the Daily Sketch suggested of Brandreth "a new Frost is born" with another newspaper headline described him as the "heart-throb of the seventies". They never saw the jumpers coming...

ITV also had a vote for **"Man of The Decade"** (10:30pm, December 30th 1969) with broadcaster Alistair Cooke choosing John F Kennedy and at the other side of the spectrum Vietnamese revolutionary leader Ho Chi Minh being nominated by novelist Mary McCarthy. Most interesting however was Desmond Morris' choice of John Lennon who agreed to an accompanying interview near his Ascot home. Lennon made many interesting points about education and the possibility of peace, while clips were interspersed of The Beatles right through the sixties starting with their début from October 1962 for the Granada-only "People and Places" through to the bed in with Yoko who was naturally also present at the filming. It's strange to think that at this point Lennon knew The Beatles were officially done although it wouldn't become public knowledge until the following April when McCartney announced he was leaving the group. Or maybe John did depending on who you listen to on what day in which trousers.

1970-74

The BBC One beat went on in **1970** with Elton John, Traffic, Labi Siffre, Livingston Taylor, CCS and Bloody Lulu going "**Into 71**" (10:55pm) but for the actual midnight hour the Beeb decided it was high old time that we return to "**The Good Old Days**" (11:50pm) which at least is a live edition from Leeds featuring the never-exhausting Norman Wisdom. ITV continued with Andy Stewart in "**The Hogmanay Show**" (11:55pm) as he's joined by Dana and the much loved within Scotland Francie and Josie played by Jack Milroy and Rikki Fulton, the latter of which would soon become a huge part of the Scottish New Year's celebrations.

Before the BAFTAs got ideas above their station one of the top prize jollies on TV was The Variety Club Awards at which the children's charity honoured British entertainers. Between 1971 and 1974 this was incorporated into BBC One's annual "**Top of The Year**" (11pm) ceremonies hosted by that nice Michael Aspel. Frankie Howard is also there again to "**Welcome 72**" as ITV stuck with the tartan-taste of the first-footing variety for "Happy Auld Year" (11:30pm) though they upped the show-biz factor slightly with 1972's cheekily titled "**At Last The 1973 Show**" (10:15pm) hosted by David Frost. Stretching to two-hours, this featured a lot of "we can sell this to America" names such as Stubby Kaye, Eartha Kitt and Ethel Merman alongside our own Jimmy Edwards, Stanley Baxter, Peter Cook and Dudley Moore. 1973's special replaced Frost for the equally dazzling Bernard Manning who brought homes "**New Year's Eve at the Golden Garter**" (11:15pm) from Manchester. Already well known for his appearances on moribund stand-up vehicle "The Comedians", Manning would soon star as the compere of the fictional **"The Wheeltappers and Shunters Social Club"** the following year which would quickly garner its own New Year's Eve specials in 1974 and 1975 due to its huge popularity at the time.

1975-79

After a few years of just settling back and showing a film BBC Two returned to the Big Ben boogie in the opening minutes of **1975** with the first 'best of the year' compilation of the serious music for serious people programme **"The Old Grey Whistle Test"** (12:03am) These collections would become a regular fixture of Two's year end plans until the late 80s and were much appreciated by younger viewers who would otherwise be stuck with the likes of 1975's **"For Auld Lang Syne"** on BBC One where the 'highlights' seem to be *"Max Boyce joins the crew of the Mumbles Lifeboat for an informal get-together at The Pier Hotel"* and that still-disgraced paedophile bothering people at Stoke Mandeville like bloody usual. He's back in the following year's **"Welcome 1977"** too alongside *"New Year's greetings from BBC stars Kojak, Starsky and Hutch, Petula Clark and from the Armed Services worldwide"* which is probably why they brought back the relative sanity of **"The Good Old Days"** (11pm) for 1977 and 1978 along with **"Celebration"** (12:01am) from BBC Scotland which offered viewers an early glimpse of the future with the charged comedy of The Krankies unleashed on the latter show.

The move away from pop to light entertainment continued as the final hours of **1979** were, like 1969, given over to a retrospective, but this time it celebrated the great television of the decade with Penelope Keith introducing **"The 70s Stop Here!"** (10:40pm) with highlights of *"some of the BBC programmes which achieved popularity, esteem or even notoriety during the decade."* There was still room for Scottish things though and **"A Toast to the 80s"** (12:01am) featured the heady mix of newsreader Reginald Bosanquet, impressionist Aiden J. Harvey and actor Bill Paterson. And, because it's still Scotland, "special guest Jim Watt with Babcock and Renfrew Pipe Band". Stanley Baxter and Fulton Mackay did similar for ITV in **"The First Day of The Year Show"** (12am)

Luckily for those who preferred their Lang Syne with a bit less of the auld, ITV provided **"The 'Will Kenny Everett Make It To 1980?' Show"** (11pm) beforehand with musical guests The Boomtown Rats, Cliff Richard, Roxy Music and David Bowie who performed a stripped down semi-acoustic version of "Space Oddity" which would be used as the basis for his 1980 No. 1 "Ashes to Ashes". One of Kenny's best ever shows, this full hour has his regular characters, guests on great self-effacing form, a Captain Kremmen animated story and a genuine sense of a great party viewers were lucky to be invited to - topped off by a clearly well refreshed supergroup made up of members from Thin Lizzy and the Sex Pistols chaotically chugging though various Christmas tunes. Not a bad way to see in a decade…

1980 - 84

And Ken was invited back to kick off the next year in **"The Kenny Everett New Year's Daze Show"** (11:50pm) where the sight of Bernard Manning being covered in green slime saw in the midnight bells. Sadly, some poor scheduling of this final series by Thames lead to the man they called Cuddly hot-footing it to Auntie Beeb by New Year 1981 and the mantle of anarchic end of year show was not taken up by anyone else.

The TV retrospective theme established in 1979 by BBC One was continued with **"Pick of 80"** (10pm) and **"Pick of 81"** (10:20pm) hosted by Barry Took showing clips from everything that has tickled the nation's fancy over the previous twelve months. **"The Good Old Days"** was once again given the 11pm slot in 1980... except for viewers in Scotland who, rather than the usual Paul Coia quiz show about hills or a six-part cartoon series about Gaelic accidents, got the first **"Scotch and Wry"** special. This was a sketch show vehicle for Rikki Fulton that would become a permanent fixture in Scotland every year until 1992. Only one year was skipped – the very next one in fact – where the nationally broadcast BBC Scotland production **"81 Take 2"** (11:20pm) took its place. Featuring many of the cast of BBC Two's new sketch show "A Kick Up the Eighties" including Rik Mayall, Robbie Coltrane and Celia Imrie there was also room for guest performers including Chic Murray and The Hee Bee Gee Bees which, as it sounds, was indeed a spoof of the Bee Gees courtesy of Angus Deayton, Michael Fenton-Stevens and Phil Pope. The trio had been part of the Oxford

Revue team, and their spoof of commercial radio had led from a live show at the Edinburgh Fringe to the long-running Radio 4 series Radio Active which had finished its first series several weeks before this.[52] Still in 1981, after Big Ben's chimes we DON'T return to Scotland for the first time in years. Instead, we head for Pebble Mill in Birmingham for **"Hi There 82!"** (12:05am) which undid any cool that may have emerged during the previous programme by scheduling Danny La Rue, Andy Williams, Norman Collier and Wall Street Crash "with a little help from the Hi-De-Hi! team." New Year's Eve on the commercial broadcaster was a poignant as ATV, Westward and Southern TV lost their franchises to Central, TSW and TVS. The first two wished their viewers goodbye with a simple continuity link but Southern went one further opting out of **"The Hogmanay Show"** for the finale **"And Its Goodbye From Us"** (11:45pm) featuring everyone who worked at the station bidding farewell as the studio faded to black and Southern's star logo drifted off into space, its famous guitar jingle echoing off eerily into the distance.

1982's offerings by BBC One lead with more bloody **"The Good Old Days"** (10:45pm) followed by **"Across the Years"** (11:45pm) hosted by John Craven and *"organised by the English Tourist Board"* before the brilliantly named **"The Big Ben Band Show"** (12:10pm) from Birmingham with Syd Lawrence and his Orchestra joined by Tina Cross and Shakatak for *"an informal but exciting mixture of music, comedy and nostalgia"*. On BBC Two at 10.35pm, newsreader Richard

---

[52] A special entitled "The Hee Bee Gee Bees Story" had also been broadcast by Radio 2 on December 19th 1981.

Baker presented his last report before pouring a glass of bubbly as he retired after 28 years. Then 1971's Hammer horror flick **"Hands of the Ripper"** (10:45pm) and more post-midnight **"Whistle Test"** (12:10am) highlights saw out the rest of the evening. ITV continued with **"The Hogmanay Show"** which left it to new kid on the block Channel 4 to bring the excitement and adventure to New Year's Eve. In just two months on air the station had already made headlines with exciting new presenters, challenging programming and a different way of thinking. So quite how that led to **"David Frost's End of the Year Show"** (11pm) with guests like Jonathan Dimbleby, Esther Rantzen and Nigel Dempster is a bafflement.

Frosty was back with the same show in 1983 too opposite Keith Chegwin, the St Winifred's School Choir and Eric Robson with *"special New Year messages from June Whitfield, Sir Peter Scott and The Rt Rev David Sheppard, Bishop of Liverpool"* on BBC One's **"Across the Years"** (11:45pm) which came live from "the Greater Manchester Museum of Science and Industry" to celebrate 1984's 'Heritage Year'. Kenneth McKellar had his traditional Scottish faddle with the Scottish Fiddle Orchestra on ITV leaving the only real surprise from BBC Two who foolishly moved their usual **"Whistle Test"** highlights show to the 23rd December running instead the enjoyably daft 1973 horror film **"Theatre of Blood"** (11:45pm) headed up by Vincent Price and a cast of top flight British acting cameos.

No more Frost in 1984, being replaced by Julia Migenes-Johnson for **"Julia Live Into '85"** (11:30pm) with *"a selection of songs from operetta, classical and music show favourites"*. At the same time, Andy Cameron and Kenneth McKellar did the usual for **"The Hogmanay Show"** on ITV with added Stutz Bear Cats. Having gone through a slightly awkward transitional period losing original host Bob Harris and a bit of its original title, "Whistle Test" was back for New Year's Eve 1984 with **"84 Whistle Test 85"** (10:50pm), a whole evening of live music including Nik Kershaw at the Hammersmith Odeon and Big Country keeping up the mandatory Scottish content live from Edinburgh. On BBC One, the comedian Tom O'Connor was **"Live Into 85"** (11:40pm) from the sparkling Gleneagles Hotel for a legendarily dreadful show in which the poet John Grieve forgot his lines, comedian Chic Murray struggled to find a camera and the pipers just… kept…. going. A late-night screening afterwards of "Singin' in The Rain" on BBC One was a welcome tonic for all viewers because… well, its "Singin' in The Rain"!

1985-89

1985 saw the start of a BBC One tradition that continues to this day – the big end-of-year chat show – and as he's already been doing admirably at 7pm three times a week it was fitting to book a bonus late-night shift for **"Wogan"** (11:15pm) meeting guests including Kenneth Williams who wrote in his famous diaries he got *"little response from a bemused audience dressed in paper hats"* adding *"the rest of the show was shapeless and ragged"*. Although he did enjoy seeing fellow guests Julie Walters, David Jason and "Bob" Lindsay. After that, no link up to Scotland with the now almost certainly not okay 1954 musical **"Seven Brides for Seven Brothers"** instead comfortably pulling viewers into '86. For people wanting something a little more swinging, they could always switch over to BBC Two's **"85 Whistle Test 86"** (8:05pm) which was stretched to five and a half hours closing around 1:45am. As 1985 had been the year of Live Aid there was much given over to Whistle Test's involvement in that with a lengthy documentary and 75 minutes of highlights. Plus, more of those exciting new music videos and from 11pm, live music from Madness at the Hammersmith Odeon in London and King from the Glasgow Barrowlands just before both acts splintered following low sales. Still, in a blaze of technological achievement viewers could tune into Radio 1 simultaneously and create a stereo broadcast. There's also a very ace, fantastic and top big headed special guest in the studio talking viewers through using their computers to send in "e-mail" requests via Prestel and "Micronet". You know they should. They really should. Thank you.

ITV changed its Hogmanay programme name to **"The New Year Show"** (11:45pm) but it was much the same kilt and dram-lifting as previous years, bar the appearance of Russ Abbot who performs his No.86 hit single "Let's Go to The Disco" before inevitably changing into CU Jimmy. Over on Channel 4, meanwhile, there's an alternative take on proceedings from Billy Connolly and Robbie Coltrane with music from Midge Ure, The Communards, Jim Diamond and Maggie Bell in **"At Last It's Hogmanay"** (11:20pm) advertised as "a song, a smile and a kick in the sporran". It was drunk and rowdy but nothing compared to **1986's** offering from the upstart fourth channel.

A live spin off from Channel 4's teatime music magazine "The Tube", **"Come Dancing with Jools Holland"** (10:45pm), was the decidedly odd beast beginning as a sitcom of sorts with the titular pianist being sporadically interrupted by Ruby Wax, Uri Geller and the team[53] from Channel 4's controversial late night comedy series "Who Dares Wins" running through some of the stunts set up for a curiously no-show Rik Mayall and Adrian Edmondson (*"Lavvies! Willies! Farts!"*, *"You forgot botties."*) Raw Sex (Simon Brint and Rowland Rivron) are a welcome sight, less so the then-Home Secretary Leon Brittan and Derek Hatton.

Eventually, the event becomes a sort of proto-Hootenanny with the now standard mix of fine but dull rhythm and blues jams in front of an invited audience of famous faces. Despite resembling Jools' current "Later..." get-togethers there's none of the slickness from those shows here and the wheels feel like they're about to fall off any second. None of this impressed the TV regulator the IBA with use of the F word and strong sexual humour leading to a number of job positions becoming vacant soon after.

The one member of the "Who Dares Wins" cast not present at all was Jimmy Mulville… possibly due to the fact he was hosting **"The New Year Show"** (11:30pm) on ITV at the same time with Muriel Gray, herself an escapee from "The Tube". There's some much-needed humour from the pair as

---

[53] Rory McGrath, Julia Hills, Phil Pope and Tony Robinson who timidly has to break through a fake wall prepared for absent Rik and Ade. Their non-appearance is never explained though it's clearly a late development as they're advertised in the TV Times and on the channel's own continuity as being guests.

they mock the trappings of the Hogmanay cabaret (*"At midnight you'll all be holding hands and singing 'Auld Lang Syne' round the auld Scots boom mic"*) before grooving to the quite hip n happening new sounds from Love and Money plus "new comedy discovery" Craig Ferguson who rants against the non-traditional nature of the show (*"I bet your mum never bought you a brown jersey for Christmas"*). Wonder what happened to him etc.

BBC Two was now clearly the place to be for the discerning rock fan with **"86 Whistle Test 87"** (7pm) presenting gig footage from a line-up including The Police, Jean-Michel Jarre, Suzanne Vega and Level 42. The New Year itself was seen in by **"86 Into 87 with Kim Wilde"** (11:35pm) featuring a spirited blast through a half decade of hits from the stage of "The Goldiggers Club in Chippenham". Wilde had been a bit dumper bound until her hi-NRG cover of The Supremes' "You Keep Me Hangin' On" in late October 1986 completely re-energised her career hitting No.2 in the UK and No.1 in America. Five more top ten hits would follow along with the festive staple "Rockin' Around the Christmas Tree" recorded with Mel Smith for Comic Relief the following year. The evening ended at half twelve with the first showing of D. A. Pennebaker's 1973 film of **"Ziggy Stardust and The Spiders from Mars"**, documenting the farewell performance of David Bowie as his well hung, snow white alter-ego.

Unfortunately, **1987** was to be the final year the whistle blew as the Test would be cancelled after one final hurrah with – ah, you're ahead of me here – **"87 Whistle Test 88"** (9:35pm) in which David Hepworth talked to Bruce Springsteen, John Peel introduced Zimbabwean music stars

The Bhundu Boys, there was a showing of the irony-free documentary **"U2 – Outside It's America"** and a final retrospective from the show's sixteen-year history. A fine ending to a very important part of British music TV. Just a shame about that live Gary Glitter concert from Bournemouth in the middle of it.

Aside from Two's marathon Whistle Test finale, **1987** marks possibly the low point of New Year TV as midnight brings a confusingly scheduled new **EastEnders** (11:30pm) on BBC One[54] and Des O'Connor on ITV "linking up" with journalist and bore Derek Jameson in Trafalgar Square. **1988** was a considerable improvement as BBC One began its seven-year association with the late Australian critic and comic Clive James whose **"On 88"** and onwards would continue each 31st December until 1994.

On BBC Two, no Whistles to be tested anymore but there's still a double bill of quality pop with **"Eurythmics Live"** (11:15pm) and the ridiculous **"David Bowie: Glass Spider"** (12:50am) There's an opportunity to look back at the great work for charity that so many celebrities didn't like to talk about with **"Comic Relief's Nose at Ten"** (10pm) showing highlights from the first ever Red Nose telly marathon. Earlier that night ITV's **"Every Penny Counted"** (8pm) had also revisited "Telethon '88" - a 27-hour "me too" equivalent that may have been the dullest thing ever transmitted up to that point. A few hours later, **Cilla's Goodbye '88"** (10:35pm) found the increasingly everywhere Ms. Black joined by Harry Enfield, Kenny Everett, Kim Wilde and Ned

---

[54] See "So Much Drama" for more details. Assuming you've read this book in the wrong order, obviously.

Sherrin although fans of shite will be pleased to know that it did still find a slot for Jim Davidson.

Channel 4 went mad with several hours of old BBC One programmes from the sixties in tribute to Billy Cotton, the retiring managing director of the Beeb. That was followed by Tony Roper's brilliant fifties set Scottish play **"The Steamie"** (9pm), **"Pavarotti Returns to Naples"** (10:30pm) and **"Aly Meets the Cajuns"** (11:30pm) with Scottish fiddle player Aly Bain hosting a Hogmanay special from the slightly more distant shores of Louisiana.

As the end of the decade drew nearer, **"Cilla's Goodbye to the '80s"** (9:25pm) was the bloated 210-minute variety special it deserved with everyone from Sir John Mills to Barry McGuigan. Alexei Sayle, Hale and Pace and Jonathan Ross represented the new breed of stars although Cliff Richard, Denis Norden and Michael Aspel were on hand to remind folks they were still watching ITV so not to get too excited.

Younger viewers might have been better off sticking with **"Eighties"** (10:15pm) – BBC Two's three-hour "rock review of the decade" produced by the arts strand "The Late Show" and featuring clips from everything from "Top of the Pops" to "Crackerjack". Meanwhile Channel 4 finished out the year with the sort of programme that would've been could only truly have been made for only one network – the fantastically naughty, innuendo-stuffed Christmas pudding that was **"Sticky New Year with Julian Clary"** (11:20pm) a live version of recent hit "Sticky Moments" – a silly and hugely enjoyable game show conceived by Clary and one of the channel's future stars Paul Merton.

"Clive James on the 80s" (10pm) on BBC One promised the condensing of *"ten years into two hours... from Brezhnev to the Berlin Wall, from Cecil Parkinson to the Big Bang"* and it pretty much delivered with a breathless mix of out of context clips and wry commentary. None of the usual guest interviews from his regular shows featured but assisting him to give out spurious awards (Stubble of the Decade, Special Award for Outstanding Contribution to The Art of Accepting an Award etc.) was model and actress Jerry Hall whose chemistry with James is slightly lower than that of a brick. Clearly, she was saving herself for a balding Australian of higher repute if her last marriage was anything to go by. Still, Kylie's here as musical accompaniment to the bells bonging twelve and "I Should Be Lucky" becomes the first song many Britons heard in this new shiny decade.

1990-94

Little change once in the nineties though with another wry sideways look back at the year in **"Clive James on 1990"** at 11pm followed by ten minutes of chimes and cheering then it's up to **"Carry on England"** to start the new year off for BBC One. Much more rockin' and a rollin' on the sister channel with a concert by those 'faces of the 90s' The Rolling Stones recorded that June up the Barcelona. ITV spared no expense with **"Live from The London Palladium. Happy Birthday, Happy New Year!"** (10:15pm) one of those slick, spectacular and a depressingly soulless shows celebrating 80 years of the beloved variety theatre. Doing their turn on the famous stage was a truly mystifying mix of "today's stars" - including Jim Dale, Bea Arthur, Michael Ball, Bobby Davro, Andrew O'Connor and Gary Wilmot - paying tribute to "heroes of yesteryear" - Judy Garland, Sophie Tucker, Jack Buchanan, Tommy Cooper and Danny Kaye – who are too dead to complain about it.

The real quality light entertainment however was over at Channel 4 with the nineties' first comedy sensation…and singer Vic Reeves who welcomes us to his **"New Year's Eve Big Night Out"** (11:35pm) which made a rare concession to celebrity guests including Mark Wingett from ITV's long-running police serial "The Bill" interrogating Reeves over his dodgy businesses and a rigged "Top Pop Singer of The Year Contest" featuring Kim Wilde and "Male Pop Star" - actually Michael Starke, better known as Sinbad from Brookside. (*"It's Large!"*) A brilliant bit of telly that was frustratingly left off the 'complete' series DVD of "Vic Reeves' Big Night Out" released in 2005 although it can now be found on the All4 on-demand service at least. This was followed by concert films featuring the spirit levels of pop Squeeze (yay!) and the soil in which chives grow UB40 (boo!).

1991 saw BBC One as ever sticking with the familiar Clive James end of the year spectacular – now extended to 90 minutes - before a brief check in with Big Ben and a message from the 'Archbish'. Presumably this is to save time getting to the late movie **"National Lampoon's Movie Madness"** (12:10am) a film that can be best described as…. on once. BBC Two have their own movie madness courtesy of a top double bill containing the first UK TV showing of **"Mad Max"** (10:05pm) and **"This Is Spinal Tap"** (11:35pm.)

ITV also put in the minimum effort with a brief New Year break between parts of 1986's **"Down and Out in Beverly Hills"** (10:50pm). Channel 4 easily committed the most elbow grease that year with an extended edition of the teatime chat show **"Tonight with Jonathan Ross"** (9:45pm) then **"As It Happens"** (10:45pm) an 'as live' fly on the wall documentary via satellite reflecting Moscow's first "free" New Year.

Altogether more memorable for television viewers was December 31st **1992** – the date which saw several regional channels going off air for the final time having lost their franchises due to a money-grabbing bidding war the previous year. For those under a certain age, the idea of ITV being divided up into small sections might seem a bit strange outside of the localised news reports at 6pm but much pride would be taken in telly franchises with TV presenters often saying people were from "Granadaland" (the North West) or "ATV-land" (the Midlands, later taken over by Central.) You'd come to know all the station idents before the programmes from London Weekend Television's line-drawing bombast, the bleepy synths of Tyne Tees, the wobbly and dream-like HTV and famously Thames reflecting itself in the water.

A few franchisees came and went in 1982 but things remained on a largely even keel until Thatcher's government pushed through the Broadcasting Act of 1990 which would remove many of the previous guidelines in a push towards deregulation. The Independent Broadcasting Authority who kept TV competitive and fair was abolished and replaced with the less strict ITC. Suddenly it became about how much money you had to bid for your channel, not quality of programming promised. Some counties kept their franchise due to lack of opposition, others had to pay through the nose to hang on. Some were confident their long standing would see them through and were shattered to learn otherwise - TVS losing to Meridian, TSW to Westcountry, TV-am to GMTV and perhaps the biggest shock of all, Thames Television being outbid by £10 million from the deep pockets of Carlton Television who would use this as a base to expand into other stations creating the amorphous blob that is the current ITV plc.

So Thames were right to feel a bit cheesed off as they said their final goodbyes in **"The End of the Year Show"** (10:45pm) featuring *"Highlights from 25 years of light entertainment and drama from Thames Television"* which felt like the television equivalent of an ex reminding you what you were letting go as it counted down its final 75 minutes on air with clips including "The Naked Civil Servant", "The Sooty Show", "Rumpole of the Bailey", "Wish You Were Here...?", "The Wind In The Willows", "The Kenny Everett Video Show", "Mr Bean" and "Minder", followed by a final goodbye from Richard Dunn, the channel's Chief Executive and a final montage backed by The Tourists' cover of "I Only Want To Be With You".

And then it was all over. ITN were next to see in the New Year bongs before Chris Tarrant appeared in Trafalgar Square to see in the new station with Take That, Frank Skinner, some Chippendales and a bloke called McCartney and his missis. Did he know everything was about to change about commercial TV? And was that his final answer? Only time would tell...

Elsewhere, more Clive James on BBC One, a Rab C Nesbitt special **"Home"** (11:30pm) before Sandra Bernhard's **"Without You I'm Nothing"** concert film (12:20am) on BBC Two and Channel 4 trusted its new hit series to see out the year with the 90-minute live **"Big Breakfast End of Year Show"** (11:30pm) a late but not especially lewd edition of its hugely successful new morning show. And on the new UK Gold there's an **"In Concert Special"** (12am) where viewers are invited to "see in the New Year" – yep with you so far – "with some choice highlights" – my favourite kind – "from Gary Glitter's recent UK tour" – oh for fu….

Best quickly jumping forward to **1993** and BBC Two greet the New Year with the first **"Jools Holland's Hootenanny"** (12am) featuring Sting, the Gipsy Kings and Sly and Robbie. Originally spun off from the post- "Newsnight" arts and culture strand "The Late Show" (hence the "Later" tag), the "Hootenanny" would steadfastly stick to its midnight slot for several years before becoming the 11pm-ish slot behemoth in 2002, where it remains to this day.

Clive James continued running down the year on BBC One assisted this time by Louise Lombard from the popular drama "The House of ~~Idiot~~ Elliot" unless you're North of the Border in which case you got a transfer of Radio Scotland's football-based sketch show **"Only an Excuse?"** (10:30pm) which would continue until 2020. This had replaced the traditional "Scotch and Wry" Hogmanay specials as Rikki Fulton instead spun off that series' dour reverend I M Jolly in **"Tis the Season to Be Jolly"** (11:20pm), one of a number of great New Year sitcom specials solely focused on the character.

Channel 4 returned to their concept of sticking cameras in different countries as the **"New Year's Eve Triple Whammy"** followed midnight around the world beginning with Cape Town at 10pm then Prague at 11pm and Dublin at 12pm. And on satellite you could say hello to '94 with **"Terminator 2: Judgment Day"** on Sky Movies, **"Lou Grant"** on The Family Channel and an eighties **"Music Spectacular"** courtesy of UK Gold back when such a thing might be quite unique. And ITV once again failed to bother, sticking out an evening of films with **"Bonnie and Clyde"** (11:30pm) taking us into the new year.

Clive James put in his final New Year's appearance for BBC One in **1994** before heading back off to ITV but the following **"Hogmanay Live"** (12:10am) invites you to stick around for Paul Coia, Runrig and "members of the Strathclyde Police Pipe Band". Two bursts of footage from an ill-advised **"Woodstock '94"** (10:30pm, 1am) sandwich **"The Second Annual Jools' Hootenanny"** (12am) with guests Steve Winwood, Kirsty MacColl, Shane McGowan and Blur joined for "Parklife" by Phil Daniels. Over on Channel 4 more music with the **"New Year Jam Down"** and **"When Johnny Cash Went to Glastonbury"**. Hope he played some music when he was there. Seems a waste otherwise.

1995-98

Angus Deayton takes over from Clive James to provide much the same service in **"The End of the Year Show"** (11pm) on BBC One from a glorious clock-based set supposedly from the inside of Big Ben, joined by his "One Foot in The

Grave" co-star Richard Wilson, his fellow "Alexei Sayle's Stuff" co-star…erm, Alexei Sayle and rhythmic dance troupe Stomp who he doesn't seem to have worked with at all sadly. Until now anyway. **"Hogmanay Live"** (12:10am) returns after with the power duo of Gordon Kennedy and Lorraine Kelly introducing Edwyn Collins, Big Country, Eddi Reader and Gary Glitt…you know what never mind.

On BBC Two, **"The Third Annual Jools' Hootenanny"** is preceded by a TOTP2 special titled **"Britpop: Then and Now"** (11:30pm) which celebrates a year of some indie getting in the chart as clips of Menswear, Cast and Supergrass rub shoulders with The Hollies, The Kinks and Them There Beatles. Supergrass were also on Jools' show playing a blistering "I'd Like to Know" in front of rotten old Eric Clapton who I hope questioned every single decision he'd made since 1970 in that moment. Channel 4 weren't letting Jools claim all the New Year boogies however as Mark Radcliffe and Jo Whiley hosted **"The White Room"** (11:15pm) saw viewers into 1996 with a top tier line-up including Oasis, David Bowie, Lou Reed and Pulp. Shame it'd be cancelled before the next New Year came round.

And what a New Year **1996** was with the Spice Girls…but also sadly Lee Hurst joining Angus Deayton at 11pm ahead of **"Hogmanay Live"** from Edinburgh Castle, now thankfully free of seventies sex offenders. And it's all rockin' and slash or rollin' on Two with two specials from 1968 – **"The Rolling Stones' Rock and Roll Circus"** (10:55pm) and **"Elvis – the 68 Comeback Special"** (1:15am) either side of "**Jools' Hootenanny"** headlined by the Manic Street Preachers, Paul Weller and…sigh, Mick Hucknall. Thankfully there's also stars of tomorrow Kenickie and Tony Ferrino to calm our jangled nerves. ITV gave an hour over to **"The Bob Downe Special"** at 10:15pm with Mark Trevorrow's cheesy, lounge singing creation Downe getting a proper big light entertainment bonanza with music, comedy and dancing, all performed in a huge studio. Guests include the magnificent Anthony Newley who's in London to star in the musical of "Scrooge" and clearly having a ball being let back on the telly for a bit, joking and singing "The Candy Man" with Laurie Holloway's orchestra. Next Ant and Dec come on for some stilted jokes about "confirmed bachelors" before all three sing "Lady Marmalade" and finally Martine McCutcheon gamely runs through "Don't You Want Me" and a wacky, banter-filled version of Dean Friedman's "Lucky Stars" inelegantly seated on beanbags.

At his peak during the retro nostalgia craving for the 1970s, Downe is clearly a loving parody of that era and yet here it felt like nobody can decide if this was a genuine variety show or a parody of one. For such a clearly lavish production it feels strange it went out after 10pm on New Year's Eve. ITV then reverted to type with a quick trip to Trevor McDonald seeing in the New Year around a showing of the dismal Eddie Murphy vehicle **"The Golden Child"**.

Channel 4 once again brushed off **"As It Happens"** – this time taking several visits to Birmingham City Hospital for live coverage of how they cope over New Year's Eve with Drs Phil Hammond and Tony Gardner as part of its "Doctors and Nurses" season. It's preceded by an episode of the brand new **"The Adam and Joe Show"** (11:15pm), a cult comedy, pop culture and toy renditions of famous TV programmes and movies hodgepodge hosted by Adam Buxton and Joe Cornish - both of whom would be back in **1997** for a much more exciting one-off: **"Adam and Joe's Fourmative Years"** (10:10pm) This was a special charting the journey of Channel 4 as it hit its fifteenth anniversary from the opening line-up - spoofed here by Adam and Joe in toy form seeing "Countdown" and immediately falling asleep – to the present day. Buxton and Cornish clearly relish the chance to talk about all this old guff like pretentious 'art happening' "Club X" and "Minipops" with its inappropriately sexual pre-teen versions of current hits or forgotten fluff like "The Pocket Money Programme", "Surf Potatoes", "Trak Trix" and "Watch This Space" with huge affection.

Regular characters the Vinyl Justice squad look at the channel's early pop output including "The Tube", "Ear Say" (with the "notorious" Gary Crowley), "Whatever You Want" featuring a barely grown Wham! and the "Malibu World Disco Dance Championships 1983" with Leeeeeeeee John. Adam's late father Nigel "BaaadDad" Buxton talks viewers through the naughtier programmes in the back catalogue such as 1986's "Naked Yoga", the 1993 documentary "Sacred Sex" and "The Very Hot Gossip Show" featuring the Kenny Everett dancers doing much like they had on that series but with more close-ups on wiggling bums. On that same tack, the infamous "red triangle" late night 'culture' films are mentioned as is the channel's commitment to post-midnight experimental video art (*"There's a thin line between art and complete bollocks, see if you can guess which is which"*) and "suicidally grim drama". A treat for fans of archive telly, swearing toys and gleefully daft jokes, this is a love letter to a unique broadcasting period and a Channel 4 that's depressingly unrecognisable in its current form.

As if to underline where the station was headed, **"TFI 1998"** followed immediately after at 11pm hosted by a clearly unravelling Chris Evans. Launched in February 1996, "TFI Friday" quickly established itself as a must-watch show with lots of big ideas plus the biggest, hippest guests of the day and the most in demand alternative music live. By New Year's Eve 1997 though the wheels had very truly fallen off, with Evans opening the show telling a 'fun' story about throwing up. *"I'm drinking for a good cause"* says Chris to his whipping boy producer Will, *"what cause?"* he replies, *"...cause I'm an alcoholic"* comes the grim and probably truthful reply.

At least the guests are fun including Melinda Messenger, a model turned presenter who had experienced a wave of fame due to being funny and genuinely likeable even under the onslaught of jokes about her sizable breasts[55]. It's no surprise that a year on from this she would already have her own chat show. Sadly, it was on Channel 5 so nobody knew.

At least we've music and kicking off this "review of 1997" is Ocean Colour Scene with…a song from 1996. As if to service Evans' ego they play "The Riverboat Song" - i.e., the song that plays when anyone walks onto the set on "TFI Friday". As mild compensation they later return to perform the more recent "Hundred Mile High City". Also here are Mark Owen running through his mostly failed first attempt at solo success

---

[55] The breast references continued with a segment meeting people who have "made a change in 1997" which is mostly dedicated to women who have had breast enlargement surgery although someone who has had surgery in order to change gender closes the section. They're confident, funny and seem comfortable in their skin, unlike Evans who doesn't know what to say so over-compensates with more babble about tits.

after Take That and, no doubt cursing their booking agent, the joyful Chumbawamba, wearing "One Hit Wonder" T-shirts, singing the still anthemic "Tubthumping"

Frank Skinner's next and the world freezes for a second when Evans asks if 1998 will be the year his mum is allowed to call him his real name (Chris Collins) again seemingly unaware that Skinner's mother has been dead since 1989. In his bluster, he tries to blame an off-screen Danny Baker but the mood is tarred and doesn't get better when Des Lynam, at the peak of his ironic hipness, arrives to talk about a great year for sport. Leading the actual count down to midnight is the actual "Countdown" clock from Channel 4's long running quiz. Auld Lang Syne is sung (a dazed Evans seems unsure of the words) then a pissed Ocean Colour Scene bellow "arse" over the final link.

Had it come the year before, this could've just about held together quite entertainingly. There are flashes of the old ideas factory as the crew have set up 1,998 alarm clocks set to go off at midnight so they don't miss it. Evans also has breakable stunt bottles to smash over guests' heads and maggots in his drawer for no apparent reason other than it'd probably be funny. A heavily trailed feature in the first and second parts is later dropped due to them over-running which was an achievement for a programme with hardly any content. "TFI Friday" would return for a short revival series in 2015 ending with a much tamer New Year's Eve special at 7:30pm but "TFI 1998" was a hangover nobody wanted to remember the following day. All of which makes Angus Deayton's antics on BBC One look positively tame. As well as **"Hogmanay Live"** (12:10am) and **"Jools' Hootenanny"** (11:55pm) with BB King and Blur again, ITV actually made an effort for the first time in years. **"Happy New Year from Edinburgh's Hogmanay"** (11pm) was a 95-minute special fronted by Anthea Turner and Phillip Schofield *"joined by 180,000 people for the UK's biggest street party"*. And to celebrate they've invited Texas, The Saw Doctors, Fred MacAulay and Space!

And new kid Channel 5 has their usual edition of **"The Jack Docherty Show"** at 11:45pm even if, between dodgy signal, regular viewership and the level of competition, its contents will remain forever secret. Going throughout the night until 4:30am is the cult sports call in show **"Under the Moon"** (12:15pm) which is still missed by many an insomniac.

After so much going on in 1997, everything was back to regular pace in **1998** - Angus on **"The End of The Year Show"** (10:45pm), **"New Year Live"** (11:40pm) offering Scottish celebrations with terrible guests (Frank Bruno, the McGann brothers and Sarah Brightman), a new message from the Archbish and a Carry On film making up BBC One's evening. Sadly its "Carry On Columbus" so you might prefer an early night instead.

As ever, the **"Hootenanny"** ploughs on with Tom Jones, Catatonia, Gomez and The Corrs (11:55pm) followed by "**Glastonbury 1998"** highlights (1:15am) Before those however is **"Mark Lamarr's New Year In"** (7:45pm) featuring the once popular comedian doing his "I don't like things" shtick around a series of totally unrelated programmes including **"The Making of Robot Wars"**, a new to terrestrial TV episode of **"The Simpsons"**, the tremendous weird short cartoon **"Rex The Runt"**, and **"A Kick Up the Archives"** a compilation of early 80s Scottish comedy. ITV's New Year's Eve is also all over the place with the combined weight of **"The Bill"**, Freddie Starr, a feature-length **"Emmerdale"**, some **"Ruth Rendell Mysteries"** and a tribute to Scottish comic actor Stanley Baxter fifteen years after LWT got rid of him. Then it's over to **"Happy New Year from Edinburgh Castle"** (11:45pm) with Jenny Powell and oh...John Leslie that lasts all of twenty minutes before its time for yet another New Year's airing of **"Down and Out in Beverly Hills"**.

Having taken Channel 4 into 1998 Chris Evans is back with **"TFI New Year"** but only for a short best of leaving a **"Eurotrash"** compilation to see in midnight followed by an Adam and Joe "Toy Movie" compendium. Channel 5 has yet more C-list karaoke in **"Night Fever"** and dull melodrama **"Stanley and Iris"**. *Sad party blower noise*

1999

And now the millennium is here to turn all of our home computers into dangerous murder machines. Might as well relax, switch on the telly and wait for it all to quietly end, eh?

ITV remember they have the qualified "New Year's Man" Clive James on hand and duly give him the two-hour special **"A Night of 1,000 Years"** ...on December 30th, where Jools and his **"Millennium Hootenanny"** also find themselves due to the all-out trousers to the floor live celebrations each channel had scheduled to see in the year 2000. Particularly egregious in ITV's case as they'd dedicate just 70 minutes to **"Countdown 2000"** (10:55pm) otherwise sticking with more necessitous items like "Casper: A Spirited Beginning", "Turner and Hooch" and "Superman 2".

Channel 4's newest star took over New Year for the rude and raucous **"FY2K: Graham Norton Live"** (11:15pm) which made "Come Dancing with Jools Holland" seem like a kids programme. That was followed by **"The Biggest Breakfast Ever"** (12:35am), an eight-and-a-half-hour edition of the morning show with Liza Tarbuck and Johnny Vaughan. And as for Channel 5, oh you know they went with a four-hour 'decades of pop' edition of **"Night Fever"** before a showing of **"Emmanuelle"**. A cruder person would label that "Suggs and jugs". But not me, I'm a good lad. Oh yes.

So, what did the BBC do to see in the apocalypse? Well…

"2000 Today" (9:15am, BBC One, December 31st) was heralded as *"The start of biggest ever live broadcast in TV history - 28 hours of celebrations as people of the world bid farewell to and welcome the new millennium."* But what did it actually feature?

Taking the gravitas and slight mania of the BBC's Election coverage – including the same host David Dimbleby – "2000 Today" was determined not to miss a second of…well, the seconds ticking down to midnight with sixty countries featured throughout the programme, starting with the South Pacific island of Kiribati. As such, the 'action' starts 14 hours and 44 minutes before midnight in the UK with Peter Sissons, Fergal Keane, Gaby Roslin and Michael "Bloody" Parkinson on hand to give out useful tips like time being a constant and they can't change things "unlike a football match…or a recorded programme".

Music features heavily and Tim Vincent is in Cardiff where both the Manic Street Preachers AND Shaky are playing gigs, Kirsty Wark checks in from Edinburgh which will soon be host to a Texas concert and there's live footage from the Pyramids as a million people watch Jean Michel-Jarre playing what Michael Buerk describes as "all that Egyptian stuff". Elsewhere, the Honeyz serenade Birmingham and in Greenwich Park "in association with British Gas" there's the Eurythmics, Bryan Ferry and sigh...Simply Red. And then there's the Dome. Not the O2 Arena but the Millennium Flipping Dome which - as we all know - cost 500 billion pounds and only showed "Blackadder Back and Forth" on a loop. Thousands flocked to its opening night where the Queen and Tony Blair watched the Archbishop of Canterbury become the opening act for The Corrs.

President Yeltsin's resignation provided a bit of actual non-millennial news and some bloke named Putin is apparently favourite for his replacement. Adding more tension is a race for who will be the first baby born in the new Millennium being overseen by medical professional Nick Knowles. The potential millennium bug problems are tracked by a breathless Peter Snow as Japan experiences two failures at nuclear power plants in Isikawa and Onagawa along with several missiles being fired from Russia. It's also testament to the months of preparation and work by IT crews all around the globe that we barely even felt the wave of change.

"2000 Today" was ridiculous, frequently filling for time and has way too much Michael Parkinson on it but it's hard not to be impressed at the sheer scale of the huge production that only an organisation like the BBC could put on with such grandeur. Nearly a hundred countries simulcast some or all of the entire broadcast with an estimated worldwide audience of 800 million people looking on in awe and wondering if that's the bloke from "Ghostwatch".

Did television get worse in the coming decade? Almost certainly. Did it still make interesting, hilarious, challenging, controversial, gripping programmes? Absolutely so.

A lot has changed in the 40 years I've focused on in this book and even more in the twenty-one since - some better, some worse. I can't deny that it's a lot harder to get excited about television in the modern age even though it's never been easier to tap into broadcast streams from anywhere in the world, share rare videos or watch twenty things simultaneously. That said as I wrote this book in late September 2021, a (thankfully non-fatal) disaster at TV company Red Bee Media took out Channel 4, Channel 5 and myriad other stations right in the middle of Saturday night leading to Twitter nearly exploding. I could still feel a little bit of the excitement of television not being this boring content delivery box in the corner of the room.

I still love TV - it's why I've written five books on the subject – but it feels definitely on the ropes when dealing with the onslaught on streaming media channels and while many would assume networks would strive to make more creative programming as a riposte to this, the opposite seems to be happening. But I continue to believe. Because telly really is a box of delights.

Come on, Barney dog…

Closedown

"I'll just do a quick best of for the less discerning Amazon market" he says. Two months later, it's finally finished. With my previous three Christmas TV books as guide, I reckon I've written at least 75% of this one from scratch, occasionally revising and updating entries I liked from before to make previously desperate threads into sull stories. I hope it's been interesting to track the progress of various actors, performers, genres and channels in this new format.

Thankfully 2021 was a bit better than the previous year though we still live in an uncertain awkward time. As such it did me proud to read your messages of warmth and appreciation for my books over the last two years which clearly provided some much-needed nostalgia away from the realities of today. Thank you all for that.

The best people undoubtedly shined through it all especially Christine Coulson, Shona Brunskill, Sarah and Damian Curran, Paul Abbott, Jonathan Sloman, Chris and Kylie Bate, Garreth Hirons, Phil Catterall, Sian Chatfield, Josh Tildesley, Louise Gunn, Tim Barker and Zoey Phoenix who all did their best to keep me on the straight and narrow.

A hearty hello and thank you for friendship, support and general loveliness too to Joe, Keeley and baby Maggie, Pete Prodge, Katie Kelly, Louis Barfe, Sean Howe, Lorraine Ramage, Claire and Phil, Louise Nilon, James Wallace, Matt Lee, Andy Hardaker, Paul O'Brien, Jenna, Chris and the kids, Dave Joy, Russell Hillman, Justin Lewis, Lisa and Andrew, Jason Heeley, Molly James, Paul Twist, Neil Miles, Marc, Sophie and Tilda, Jonny Mohun, John Rivers, PDT, Tim

Worthington, Darrell Maclaine, Simon Tyers, Julian and Steve, Keir, Rhys, Sebastian, Kerry, Tracey, Christopher and all the Discord folk, the podcast regulars and you for reading this book! We're all still here and that's got to mean something.

Keep watching the skis!

Your pal,

Ben Baker

October 2021

Other Books What I Done

"I Was Bored On Christmas Day: 90's Christmas Telly from Ant and Dec to Zig and Zag"

Telling the story of the nineties through the TV that we watched and the people who made it, this is a kiss under the mistletoe with the shows the defined a nation and a fumble with the things that fell through the cracks. It's an era where we said "Eh-oh" to the Teletubbies and goodbye to the Trotters, Noel Edmonds was everywhere and people nervously waited out the Millennium and the end of times it would inevitably bring. A time where mobile phones, the internet and DVD were becoming an affordable reality yet co-existed in a world where Bamboozle on Teletext, the Funfax and VHS cassette labels marked "MUM'S TAPE – SOLDIER SOLDIER – DO NOT TOUCH" were still a regular sight in many homes. It was the nineties and it feels like it happened only two minutes ago and simultaneously in another lifetime.

"Death By Stereo"

A book about the strange world of pop music with the biggest bands that never made the top ten, Irish pop from a distinctly outside perspective, the early days of Frank Sidebottom;, the UK's top 25 drinking songs, the best of Creation Records, the mysterious majesty of Australian art rock lunatics TISM, how to be a DJ, Madness and Judge Dredd - a marriage made in the IsoCubes?, why Kenickie deserved better, the least greatest Greatest Hits, Bowie, The Beatles and even the perfect funeral party! Plus more!

"Christmas Was Better In The 80s"

From the smash hits to the forgotten obscurities, it's a unique, factual yet comic look back at everything from Only Fools and Horses to Yogi Bear's All-Star Comedy Christmas Caper. It was a time before satellite or even a fourth channel to begin with! With 125 all-new mini articles, it's a fun, breezy read whether you're barmy about the box or vicarious viewer.

"Kill Your Television"

A love letter to all things televisual - taking in everything from ALF to Z Cars and paying tribute to the programmes, presenters, sounds and strange spin-offs that made the flashing square box in the corner of the room great.

"Ben Baker's Fun Book for The Apocalypse"

As series of silly things to do in lockdown or a very rainy day with all new quizzes, games and "procraftination" to try.

"The Comedy Cash-In Book Book"

A personal look at what made the spin-off comedy book so popular in the UK between the 1970s and 1990s. From Monty Python's exceptionally influential 'Boks' through to the unique, brilliant humour of Harry Hill taking in Morecambe and Wise, The Goodies, Kenny Everett, Saturday Night Live, The Young Ones, Lenny Henry, Smith and Jones, Harry Enfield, Mr Bean, Reeves and Mortimer, Father Ted, Lee and Herring, The League of Gentlemen and many more along the way. It's also got quite a lot of jokes in it. A must for anyone who likes British comedy.

"Talk About the Passion: New Adventures in Old Pop Culture"

A best of my old pop culture fanzine "TATP" plus over thirty pages of new material from myself and Tim Worthington. Viz, Godzilla, British comics, Earl Brutus, Garfield, 1986's best toys, Newsradio, Frank Sidebottom, The Beatles, Sesame Street, TV puppets and lots more feature within!

We now conclude our broadcast day. Please remember to switch off your book.

Printed in Great Britain
by Amazon

53642845R00135